Learn To Love More :

A Course
For All Ages

Philip Snow

Dedicated to those who dream of a world filled with love

CONTENTS

1. COURSE INTRODUCTION

Lecture 1: Course introduction and objectives

Hello and welcome to your course, helping you to learn to love more.

My name is Philip Snow, and I'll be your instructor throughout the course.

Let's get straight into this, and the first thing I'd like to teach you is:

You are the very embodiment of love.

You are the very embodiment of love.

You are the very embodiment of love.

How would I know that? Well, I've made it my life mission to inspire people to love more. And I've studied, and I've practiced, at various stages of my life, whatever it takes to understand the theory and the practice of love. I've learnt that we're all embodiments of love. And love should be what makes the world go round.

The understanding that we're all embodiments of love is not common amongst people. I've studied and experienced aspects of life which not very many people have. Now, after many decades of learning and experience I'm confidently able to say that you, yourself, personally, are the very embodiment of love.

As I'm setting out to help you realize that you're an embodiment of love, I'm not claiming that I'm a perfect role model of an embodiment of love, but at least I'm working on it. It's a process, and any progress you can make in that process can make a huge difference in your life.

And at least I feel I'm qualified now to fulfill my life mission by explaining to as many people as possible how it's possible to love more, and what will happen when you do.

The course is made up of ten sections with a number of lectures in each. Each section of the course will start with a brief introduction in which I'll set the context for the section, and will end with a brief conclusion to enable you to see exactly what you are learning from the course and can now apply in your life, and what the benefits are going to be.

There are quizzes for you to answer, so that you can check that you're picking up the key points, and there are extra resources of various kinds in the Resources section of many of the lectures.

I'll start by giving you a number of simple practical exercises which will help you to learn to love more, straightaway. That's because I'm thinking you might be wanting to get some immediate results before you decide to wade through the whole length and breadth and depth of what I'm going to explain in order for you to realize in full, and put into practical, everyday use, that you, truly, are an embodiment of love.

Here's an exercise you can practice straightaway and get an immediate result, and adopt as a lifelong practice.

Go to someone, someone close to you or someone you've never met before. Say something appropriate, it doesn't matter what. Whilst the connection between you lasts, find something about that person that you could say you love. It could be anything. It could be something about the way they look, the way they speak, the difference between yourself and them in any way, their shyness, their openness, it could be something for which you might have some compassion, something which reflects or strengthens a commonality or unity between you, something you admire, something that makes you smile, particularly something that you realize is making your eyes and your whole face and your voice soften, which will suggest that your heart is warming to them.

You need to find something about them that you feel you can love. It's not that hard. Everyone is lovable, more than most people realize, and one of the purposes of this course is to show how true this is.

Preferably, at the beginning of your exchange with someone, smile. You'll feel relaxed and more positive. Even though this isn't essential for this exercise, at least it's a good way of opening the exchange.

If you manage to see something about that person that you love in some way, to some degree. and it's really very easy, see if you get a good reaction of some sort from the other person, a smile, or a softening in their body language, in some way. Sometimes you will, sometimes you won't, but if you don't, remember that that's probably more to do with them than it is to do with you.

If you've never consciously practiced this before, it's something that will help you to love more. A deliberate giving of some aspect of love.

Now do that with everyone you meet, always.

You do have to put in a bit of effort into it, but it's not so hard. If you don't find something to love about someone, I'd venture to say you're not putting your heart into it enough. Alternatively, just decide that you love them anyway.

In the Resources section of this lecture you'll find a worksheet you can make copies of. The purpose of this is to keep a record of your experiences and progress. Make notes of what you saw in a person that you haven't been so conscious of previously, how that made you feel, and whether you got a reaction from the other person, and what it was.

Resources:

Worksheet

Make notes about your experiences of finding something to love about people you engage with in some way.

Making notes will reinforce your practice of finding something to love about people, and opening your heart to people.

Aim to make notes of at least 10 separate instances of such experiences. The more, the better; then you can see your progress over time, verify the positive value of the practice, and make it into a good habit.

1. What was the meeting? For example, talking with a stranger on the street; someone at work; someone you already know; being served by someone in a store, or restaurant; or, just observing someone, somewhere.

2. What did you find in that person that caused your heart to open to them in some way? For example, something about they way they look, they talk, they behave; something they said, etc., etc.

3. What particular feeling did that give you? A good connection? A general sense of liking them? Make you smile/laugh? Thankfulness? Acceptance of the person? Some sort of recognition of difference, of similarity, of some quality or other?etc., etc.

4. How did it make you feel physically? You relaxed your body language? Your voice changed? Your eyes/face softened? You smiled/laughed? etc., etc.

5. How did they react to you? They relaxed their body language?
   Their voice changed? Their eyes/face softened? They smiled/
   laughed? etc., etc.

Now let's go on to the next lecture to start really opening your heart.

———————————

2. OPENING YOUR HEART

Lecture 1: Love is where the heart is

The old expression goes, "Home is where the heart is". Wherever your heart is, you'll feel at home. I'm saying "love is where the heart is", and that has a double meaning.

Firstly I'm saying that love is home, and as we go on through the course, I will explain that more.

The second meaning is that love is experienced mainly in the heart.

A biologist will say that the heart cannot have feelings. That's true, but I'm not talking about the physical heart; I'm talking about the spiritual heart which is located close to the physical heart, more in the centre of the chest. It's an energy centre, not really a physical thing. It's normally called the heart chakra, and is well-known to the ancient spiritual traditions especially in the East. But I'm not going to go into such details in this course. Suffice it to say what all of us say, "my heart is full of love, my heart is bursting with love, my heart is broken", and so on, and we use the heart shape to denote love. So let's agree that the heart is where we experience love.

The degree to which we can experience love in our heart is determined by how open our heart is. Some of us have an open heart, some of us have a closed heart. Some are said to have a heart of gold, some of us are said to have a heart of stone. If we're going to experience more love, we have to have an open heart and be warm-hearted.

How open do you feel your heart is? Can you feel your heart react? How readily does your heart melt in response to something that makes you feel love? How readily do you cry in response to something that makes you feel love, whether it makes you feel happy or sad?

However open your heart is, it's possible for it to open more. The more open your heart is, the more love you can feel.

So, before we do anything else, let's open our heart some more. This is the purpose and the objective of this section. I'm going to offer you a number of techniques for opening your heart.

Lecture 2: Consciously Opening Your Heart

Consciously opening your heart is something you can do almost all the time. This can rapidly produce results, in the form of you feeling that your heart is opening.

In the introduction to the course I offered you a technique you can use whenever you're with another person. I hope by now you've experienced that it can have an immediate effect in showing you how you can love more. I'd ask you now to be conscious of how it makes your heart feel. The more you do this the more you will be aware of your heart opening as part of the process of extending your love more.

Other ways of opening your heart are probably best left to your own personal inclinations or preferences.

For example, my preferences include thinking about or engaging with someone who makes me feel very loving. Indulging myself in that feeling of loving enables me to feel my heart opening.

Also there are particular types of music that make me feel very loving. These would normally be pop music, probably ballads, in which it's either the words or the music or both which have a great effect on me. I could name many singers and composers, to whom I would sit down to listen, or have playing in the background. For example, Dionne Warwick, Dusty Springfield, Neil Diamond, George Michael, Agnetha Faltskog - the blonde lady from Abba, Leona Lewis, Whitney Houston, the Righteous Brothers, lots more singers like that. Vangelis, as a composer. Mendelssohn, Mozart, Mascagni. Not all of these people's songs or compositions, just some particular ones and sometimes just part of the song, or part of the instrumental like a particularly beautiful saxophone trill, such has in Vangelis' love theme for the first Blade Runner movie, and in George Michael's 'Careless Whisper' song, and Gary Barlow's "Million Love Songs". Some of the spoken words in the melancholic Blade Runner movie (I love melancholy) have the same effect on me, where the plight of the artificial, human-like Replicants who have only a four-year lifespan, moved me so deeply the first time I saw the movie that I carried that beautiful, blissed-out feeling with me for three days afterwards. Some of the script was wonderful, such as when the leader of the replicants, a really brutal guy named Roy Batty, when he was dying, said, "All these moments will be lost, in time, like tears in rain." To which Harrison Ford the policeman Blade Runner said, "All he'd wanted are the same answers the rest of us want, where do I come from, where am I going, how long have I got?" I go on to YouTube specifically to listen to things like that, that make my heart melt, leaving me in a dreamy mood. Or I'll have it playing in the background whilst I'm doing something else.

I love music in a minor key. Music in a minor key evokes melancholy, longing and sadness. It stirs the love-sick heart, stirs the sorrow, in my case the heart that wants to see more love in the world. Rachmaninov's Piano Concerto Number 2 in C minor has always been one of my favorites. It has some exquisitely beautiful piano sequences in it.

Being in nature can open my heart. I love looking at wildflowers, which can look so fragile and beautiful and yet are so resilient to the weather and the seasons. Cultivated flowers too can be so beautiful. Roses, the combination of their beauty and their fragrance, are good enough to stir my heart, and make me want to just look at them and enjoy the feelings I get. Even a photograph of a rose Is enough to make me think I can smell the scent of it wafting over me.

I like doing things for people; I always have done. It makes me feel good to do things for people.

A word of caution here, though: doing things for other people is not always the best exercise for opening the heart, as we're talking about at the moment. Doing things for other people can have its problems. People can want too much from you, or they may feel obliged to give back in return. The best way I find to give without risking such problems is to give anonymously, for example to a charity that does the kind of work that stirs my heart, such as in the case of a natural disaster where one feels compassion for the victims. Or being considerate to someone, such as giving way to someone in a store, or in traffic. But that's not to say that giving to people, being helpful to people, isn't always a good thing to do; I'm simply saying that one needs to consider what one is doing when one gives of oneself to people. It may not open your heart, nor theirs. We'll be going into this some more, later in the course.

What sort of things stir your heart? Can you spend more time indulging yourself in such things? There's a worksheet in the resources section of this lecture and you can write down the things you find stir your heart. You could make a habit of looking at it sometimes during the day, to prompt you to do something to stir your heart; and having a list of things will help you find something you can do there and then.

We may not be able to spend all our time indulging the feelings of our heart, but we could spend quite a lot more time than we do now. It's so pleasurable that we might want to do it all time, and that should tell us something, maybe that we want our life to be more pleasurable, more heart centered. I suggest that we do it as much as we can and certainly not feel guilty about using our time that way. I reckon it's probably the best investment of time we can make. And how many of those people we love would object to being the focus of our love a little bit more?

Resources:

WORKSHEET

Make a list, using categories, of things that stir, warm and open your heart; make time, preferably every day, to indulge your heart with these heart-stirrers, so that your heart will open more, and become more responsive to such stimuli.

Categories, and sub-categories, might include, e.g., people, pets, music, movies, nature, creative activities, being kind, being helpful, beauty, skills, processes, etc., etc., etc.

Lecture 3: Unconsciously Opening Your Heart

What do I mean by saying, "unconsciously opening your heart"? Or I could say "subconsciously".

You know, or at least you've heard, or read, that we have a subconscious part of our mind. Mostly, we have no idea what this part of our mind is, and what goes on there. Wouldn't we just like to know?

Later on in the course I'll suggest where this subconscious part of the mind is, and how we can get access to it, and use it. (Section 5)

For the moment, though, I'd like to suggest that a lot more goes on in our subconscious mind than we realize, and that much more of our life is orchestrated from our subconscious mind than we have any idea of. I'd even go so far as to suggest that the *main direction* of our lives is determined from our subconscious mind.

Without, for the moment, understanding how this part of our mind works, we can use it for some specific purposes such as opening our heart.

I feel fairly safe in saying that your subconscious mind already knows that you want to open your heart more, because you have chosen to do this course, and your subconscious is already helping you to open your heart. Perhaps it even brought you to this course before you were consciously aware of the course. Perhaps you were unconsciously wanting to love more. Or consciously wanting to love more and your subconscious mind directed you to this course, in some way that you thought you did for yourself, such as looking for a course like this online.

You can help your subconscious mind to help you even more by showing your subconscious mind that you are ready and willing to apply yourself to opening your heart. Your subconscious mind will respond by helping you more, in a great variety of ways.

The way in which your subconscious works is according to one of the laws of nature called "the principle of least action" which means that it will choose the simplest, easiest and fastest method available to it. Like water running downhill, it finds the easiest way it can find. And it happens automatically, as part of the actual processes of life, using the day-to-day machinations of what's going on in life. Believe it or not, you opening your heart is part of the natural processes of the whole of life, which I will explain more about it later.

For the moment I ask you simply to write to your subconscious mind an affirmation of your intention to open your heart. This will, in effect, create a contract between your conscious self and your unconscious self that you'll pay attention to the process, in all its aspects, through which your heart is opening and you'll cooperate and collaborate with the doings of your subconscious or unconscious self on your behalf.

For example, you might write, "I ask my subconscious mind to assist me in my efforts to open my heart. I pledge to pay attention to any circumstances, events, opportunities, indications, intuitions and so on that I become aware of, that my subconscious mind might be orchestrating on my behalf. I pledge to cooperate and collaborate with such things so that the opening of my heart can be facilitated with the least of effort and maximum of success. I thank my subconscious mind for helping me to open my heart." You could make it a lot simpler than that, and probably should do. And then you should read it out loud to your subconscious self at least once a day, in a spirit of respect and gratitude.

You'll find in the resources section of this lecture a worksheet that you can copy. You can write your affirmations on it, and carry it around with you. By all means change your affirmations if you think you can improve on them. Also write on your worksheet details of any circumstances, events, opportunities, indications, intuitions and so on that you think might have been brought to you by your subconscious mind. And write details of what you did to make use of these, and what results came of them. This will reinforce your knowing that your subconscious mind is accessible to you and is ready and willing to help you, and is always extremely effective.

Resources:

WORKSHEET

Affirmation/Intention

Compose an affirmation or intention, addressed to your unconscious or subconscious mind, as your part of a two-way contract which you will honor.

You are asking your unconscious/subconscious mind to help you to open your heart more, and you are committing yourself to pay attention to whatever you see or feel your unconscious/subconscious is doing to help you; to work with those things; to make notes about what those things are; how you are working with them; what has been the outcome, immediately, and over time, etc.

Also, thank your unconscious/subconscious mind for the help it is, and will be, giving you.

Read this affirmation aloud to your unconscious/subconscious mind at least once a day whilst you are going through this process of opening your heart more.

Change/add to/update this affirmation/intention at any time, as you wish.

Lecture 4: Experiencing Unity to Open Your Heart

I'm making a separate lecture for this because I consider it to be very important. Later in the course, I'll go into why and how expressions and experiences of unity in love can be hugely effective for you in your day-to-day life, but for the moment this fits into our exercises for opening your heart more.

Some years ago, 20-odd years ago, someone whom I respected a great deal told me that 'unity' could be experienced as "seeing yourself in the world, and the whole world in yourself".

What this meant was that whatever you may see in other people, you can also see within yourself; not necessarily to the same degree, but to some degree, however small, in every single respect you can think of. This would be true no matter how different the other people are to yourself, in terms of culture, race, religion, nationality, gender, behavior and so on. If you consider this deeply enough, you realize that essentially we are all at least very similar, if not the same, and these similarities are enough to engender a sense of humanity being a single, very large family, a unity, of which we truly are a member, and we are all equal in the most important respects.

Similarly, seeing the whole world in yourself, means looking deeply into yourself and seeing that you, yourself, contain all the attributes and qualities of all people everywhere, again not necessarily in the same degree or combinations of attributes and qualities, but enough to say that we are all essentially, fundamentally, the same. We may not like that idea, but if we consider it deeply enough, we will find that It is true, and it would be good to face up to the fact.

This inherent unity which we share with all other people is something which we can use to open our heart. We can do a very great deal more than that with this unity, as we will see later in the course. When we know that other people are essentially very much the same as ourselves, we have a very strong basis for engendering good relationships with other people, no matter how different they may appear to be on the surface. So often, we use the perceived *differences* to justify keeping our hearts closed towards other people. When we recognize and acknowledge our *essential unity*, we know there is no justification for keeping our heart closed.

Open your heart to everyone you meet, regardless. Obviously the other person or people may not do the same. But opening hearts starts here, with us.

Lecture 5: Evidence That Your Heart Is Opening

If you haven't been aware of your heart being open or opening more, you can take your attention to it and feel what it's feeling like.

Feelings of love are not concentrated into the heart centre, that's where *most* of the sensations may be felt, but they wash over oneself so the whole of your awareness tends to get overwhelmed by such feelings. The degree to which one feels overwhelmed is a pretty good indicator of how open your heart is. If your love makes you cry, then obviously the feeling is affecting your entire nervous system. And that explains why love can also be a powerful healing energy for you; more on that later.

For our purposes here, it would be good for you to develop a keen appreciation of how much your heart reacts to the sensations of love in all their manifestations, pleasant or otherwise - by which I also mean sadness, grief and so on.

Usually there will be a sensation of softness, quietness, peaceful-ness, even blissfulness, feelings which can feel very pleasant even though they may have the overtones of sadness, etc. One may feel like crying, and crying of course can be an expression of joy as much as it can be of sadness. Even depression can be a really pleasant feel-ing, making one indulge in the feeling of it.

We're all probably familiar with the whole array of feelings associ-ated with love. What we are looking for here is a more responsive heart, one which expresses love more freely, one which we know is expressing love more freely. We will know that we are expressing love more freely when we are feeling the sensations of love in our heart more readily, more acutely, more overwhelmingly.

The heart doesn't only feel love in what we think of as the positive, uplifting qualities of love, such as togetherness, acceptance, generosity, joy, forgiveness, caring. It can also feel what we can consider, perhaps wrongly, to be more negative qualities of love such as sadness, grief, compassion, sympathy, empathy, loneliness, regret, melancholy and such things like that. Gosh, there's a lot of those, isn't there. But it's important to be able to feel such feelings appropriately, so that one can respond to them appropriately.

The heart doesn't feel such emotions as anger, fear, hate, frustration, anxiety and suchlike. These and various other emotions are felt in other energy centers, up and down the body.

Incidentally, and a word of caution here, you may find that as your heart opens more, you become more aware of feelings of anger and fear and frustration etc. You are becoming more aware of all of your feelings. However, this is a good thing, and you'l find these more negative feelings will gradually dissipate as you love more.

The main thing here is to recognize what's going on in your heart. What is *causing* things to go on in your heart is not the point here. The point is to cultivate your heart so that it can express love more freely.

In the resources section of this lecture (see Page 15) there's a worksheet which will enable you to keep a record of how much more freely you are expressing love as time goes on.

I suggest you make copies of the worksheet and complete one at the end of each month.

Worksheet: How Open Is My Heart?   Date: ___________________________________

How open is your heart in response to:

(make your own list of categories, also sub-categories if desired, of e.g. people, pets, places, music, movies, books, creative activities, nature, etc whatever stirs, warms and/or opens your heart)

Evaluate using this 1 – 5 range.

Note: Your first/baseline evaluation is where you started from at the beginning of the course. For your baseline evaluation, make all values 2 and then re-evaluate after e.g. 1 month, 3 months, 6 months, 1 year, **relative** to that starting point.

	1	2	3	4	5

How much do you do, of the activities you enjoy? (make your own list of specific activities)

	1	2	3	4	5

How well are people relating to you? (make your own list of e.g. family, friends, work colleagues, strangers in the street, customers, service staff, social media, etc)

	1	2	3	4	5

Lecture 6: Section Conclusion

In this section we've looked at the importance of opening your heart more so that your love can flow more freely. We've looked at various ways in which you can consciously make your heart open, and ways in which you can unconsciously or subconsciously make your heart open.

We've looked at ways in which you can have a new appreciation of how you can relate to other people in a heartfelt way, and recognize that your understanding of yourself in relation to other people can give you a very good basis for a sense of unity, togetherness, commonality and equality despite all the differences that might make us think how difficult it is to relate to other people.

We have seen that our ability to love has much more to do with ourself than with other people. There should no longer be any sense of judging other people as essentially different, or in some way inferior or superior, thus creating barriers that even love can't overcome. The main barriers to overcome are the doors to your heart and the windows out of your heart once you are in there.

To overcome these barriers is mainly a question of desiring to do so, and practicing techniques such as I have offered you to enable you to open your heart. You can reinforce your practice by keeping notes of what you have been practicing and the results you have noticed. And I've provided resources to encourage and enable you to do that.

---

3. UNDERSTANDINGS AND EXPERIENCES OF LOVE

Lecture 1: Section Introduction

The basis for my course is my understanding, based on the knowledge I've gained and the experiences I've had, that love is a lot more than most of us think it is - and that if we access and express more of the love that's naturally here within us, we can transform our own lives for the better and transform the world around us at the same time.

This course is also based firmly on my understanding, again based on my knowledge and experience, that *we ourselves* are a lot more, a very great deal more, than we normally think we are and this is true of all of us, and probably always will be; this course will help you to access a lot more of who you really are.

I'm going to introduce some ideas that you'll already be familiar with but which you may have some doubts or confusion about, and need more knowledge about. I'm going to help you resolve those doubts or confusion and provide that more knowledge. As I go along I'll give you references to other sources and resources of this knowledge and descriptions of my own experiences to back up what I'm saying.

I could say that I've been working on this course for most of my life, because I recognized at the age of 12, back in 1957, that people don't love each other enough, and I resolved at that time to spend the rest of my life "sorting that out". Quite an ambition for a 12 -year-old! At the time of publishing this I'm 75 years old so you can see it is taking me all of my life "to sort this out". And what this means is, given so many years of being conscious of this mission of mine, I've been able to accumulate the knowledge and experience to enable me to do this effectively and authentically. And of course I now have the use of technology that enables me to broadcast this course world-wide, which is great!

During the course I'll explain more about what I've been doing in my life and where I am and what I'm doing today.

In this section I'm going to start explaining what my understanding is of what love is and how deep 'love' really goes. I'll explain my understanding of why we don't already love as deeply as we could. And then I'm going to make a case for saying that we really do want to love more. And from that point onwards I'll introduce quizzes, worksheets and practical exercises so that you can begin to take what I'm explaining into your own understanding and apply it into your own life in practical, positive ways.

Most of the course will provide you with practical understanding; that is, I'll explain ways in which you can apply your new understanding into your everyday life. In that way you'll be able to access love much more deeply than before, and you actually will love more in your life and experience for yourself the many more good things that'll happen when you're loving more.

As well as the practical applications of love I'll be going into more of the theory of love, and also discussing some of the areas of our lives in which more love is needed; but most of the course will ask you to apply love in practical ways so you can experience the benefits that I am asking you to expect as you love more.

When you're ready let's go on to the next lecture.

Lecture 2: What Love Is

I'd like to explain my understandings and experiences of love; under-standings which I've gathered over many years, and experiences I've had in relation to those understandings.

Many of my understandings will be familiar enough to you but also controversial for many people. I don't want to go too deeply into theory at this stage, because we might start getting bogged down. I'm adding resources to this lecture to give you the opportunity to ex-plore certain areas of the understandings of love but I would ask you to go through the course completely before you return to this lecture to explore these various resources more deeply. After all, this is not purely a theoretical course; it's essentially a practical course and I would ask you to go through the course and apply the practical things that I'm suggesting so that you can have some direct experience be-fore you return to consider the theory in some depth.

I'll be discussing things mostly in non-scientific and non-religious terms but I will offer resources in scientific and religious terms. Per-sonally I don't practice any particular religion, because long ago I had cause for misgivings about the effectiveness of the church I was brought up in and I haven't had reason to think otherwise since - though I have had reason to think that the church holds some essen-tial truths. I study the teachings of Jesus, which I hold great store by, but I study *outside of* mainstream Christian Church teachings in this country, Great Britain. I'm definitely not evangelizing for any particu-lar religion, nor am I going to compare different religions' teachings about love.

It seems to me that most of the main religions *could be described* as reli-gions of love, and in some cases it's that love, in one form or anoth-er, which is considered to be the source, course and goal of the per-fect life. Inevitably I will make *some* mention of religious teachings on love, because many people are familiar with such teachings. And we can consider whether we are properly understanding, practicing and experiencing what we are having preached to us.

So, at this stage, not talking scientifically or religiously, I would like to offer you some thoughts, not necessarily my own original thoughts, though the wording might be mine, which will set the stage for what will follow in the course.

Love is a law of nature. Love is one of the most powerful forces in the universe. Love is an essential part of the creation. Love can be universal, infinite and unconditional. Love is what makes the world go round. Love is the answer. What the world needs now is love, sweet love, it's the only thing that there's just too little of. Love has creative organizing power. Love is a fundamental part of our own deepest nature. Every one of us has access to, and can experience, the full extent and depth of the love which is naturally within us, we need only to understand that it's there, where to look for it and how to express and experience it.

Love is expressed and experienced mainly through the heart. The extent to which our heart is open will determine how much love we express and experience. Everything and everyone can express and experience love. It's inevitable that expressing and experiencing love more deeply will involve loving everyone and everything. That deeper and deepest love is inclusive. It cannot be directed towards just one person or one thing alone, although of course one may choose to direct it towards one person or thing to a much greater degree than towards others, for reasons of one's own. And it may be in that way, in one's particular circumstances, that one would experience love in the most intense way.

First of all, though, let's look at why we don't love more, in the next lecture.

Resources:

Religious views on love:

This Wikipedia article is said (by Wikipedia) to be far from perfect, but it is an interesting compilation of the views of various religions on love:

https://en.wikipedia.org/wiki/Religious_views_on_love

Some Famous Scientists Who Believed in God

(all but one of whom are now deceased! What do today's scientists believe?)

https://www.godandscience.org/apologetics/sciencefaith.html

https://www.famousscientists.org/25-famous-scientists-who-believed-in-god/

Nicholas Copernicus

Francis Bacon

Johannes Kepler Galileo Galilei

Rene Descartes

Blaise Pascal

Isaac Newton

Robert Boyle

Michael Faraday

Gregor Mendel

William Thomas Kelvin

Max Planck

Albert Einstein

Arthur Compton

Ernst Haeckel

Erwin Shroedinger

Francis Collins

Gottfried Leibniz

Guglielmo Marconi

James Clark Maxwell

John Eccles

Louis Pasteur

Robert A Millikan

Werner Heisenberg

William Harvey

Lecture 3: Why we don't love more

The purpose of this lecture is to consider what's perhaps a surprising question: "Why don't we love more?"

It seems to me that in the English-speaking world and most of the so-called developed world there are clear reasons why we don't love more, reasons that we perhaps have lost sight of because we believe that our current way of life is the right way for an intelligent and well-adjusted society or civilization to behave.

In fact since the beginning of the Industrial Revolution in the 18th century, we have not been educated to love. We have been educated at school to be productive in the workplace. That has been the priority of school education. Love has never been considered to be a prerequisite for efficient work, though personally I would say that love very definitely has a place in the workplace when one is working as part of a group. More on that later.

In a rather similar way, religions, which one might have expected to teach the value of love, have never taught us how to love each other, and life, more deeply; rather to love or worship someone or something which is remote from our immediate reach, which is a different thing. Whilst it's true that one sees many good, loving works being done by church members in their communities, encouraged to do so by the church, the evidence, when one looks at the world at large, suggests that the religions have not taught their followers how to access and express the deepest love which the teachings that have been handed down to them suggest is vital.

Also, over the last century, since we've had movie pictures, television and another media, love has been used as a vehicle for corporations to make profit, especially through romantic story-telling, now becoming ever more sexualized, in various shades of grey. Consequently, most of today's generations associate love mostly with romance and sex. Whilst we might reasonably desire love through romance and sex, we obviously can't enjoy it with more than one person, or a very few people, at a time. Those people with whom we do not desire to have romance and sex don't readily become the objects of our love so easily. And such romantic love is often confused with lust, sexual desire, need for company, perhaps partnership, and is not necessarily given through the heart, but through our instinctive, biologically-induced imperatives to reproduce, which are often way beyond our control and demand to be satisfied - through what we call "making love".

Equally, through our preoccupation with success at work, status-seeking, self-fulfillment and material consumption, and taking into account the influences of the media, we have become habituated to a very shallow existence, one in which our sense of ourselves has become distorted into the form of a corrupted ego. Most of us now tend to identify ourselves more through our ego than through our deeper, real, naturally-loving selves. More on that later.

These things combined mean that most of us have an extremely limited idea of what love can mean in our lives, what true love is, how to access and express it, and what our potentials through love can really be.

In the following sections and lectures we will see how this can be remedied.

Lecture 4: It's natural to love

I'd just like to establish with you what we all know is true for all of us, that it's completely natural to love. We love to love. If there's one thing we all seem to want, it's love. That includes wanting to be loved but that we ourselves should love. We love to love. We love our cars; we love our pets; we love our best friend; we love our family. We love our job. We love going to the movies. We love going to the hair-dressers. We love going on holiday. We love to dance. We love going shopping; we love going to the football; we love being out in nature; we love a cold winter's day.

Okay, a lot of that isn't what we would call true love. But it does in-dicate that we love to love. We love the feeling of loving. It's one of our favorite feelings. It might even be our *most* favorite feeling.

So this suggests that loving is very deeply part of our nature. If we could spend our lives in a state of loving would we complain about it? Probably not.

If we would like to be permanently in a state of loving why do we not love all the time?   Is this because we're too busy to love, or we don't have anyone or anything to love. Is it that we find it difficult to find a suitable person or thing to love, and so we fill our lives with substitutes which give us some of the feeling of loving?

Is our heart not open enough for us to feel the feeling of loving all the time? Do we find it hard to find an object for our love, an object lovable enough to stir our heart?

Since we've established that it's natural for us to feel love and we do desire to feel love perhaps there is a way we could learn to love more.

I think there is and that's why I've made this course.

Lecture 5: How Love Makes Good Things Happen

Love, in the sense of bringing together the lover and the thing that is loved, whether that be a person or thing, or a process of some sort, is a creative, motivating law of nature.

Not only that; love also has the power to hold things together, and in balance; and it has the power to let go when the time comes. There's really no other force in the universe that has the power to do all these things.

So when we're loving, we're dealing with something that has the power to make very good things happen; and the more capably we handle this power, the more effective it will be.

What I mean, when I say, "the more capably we handle this power", is that we need to access more of the power of love than we usually do.

To do that, we're going to have to dig deeply into love and life itself for a greater understanding of love, and look at some examples of the power of love to make some really extraordinary things happen.

We'll do this over the next two sections of the course.

Lecture 5: Section Conclusion

In this section we've begun to look at what love is really all about, to set you on the path to learning how to love in a way you may never have loved before. We've begun to look at some of the theory of love but I have emphasized that this is really a practical course. The theory is merely the context in which we're working to learn to love more.

We've looked at some understandings and experiences of love. I said that I would go more deeply into this during the course and explain how I came to develop such understandings through knowledge and experience. This will enable you to do the same, though I'm not asking you to live your life the way that I've done.

We looked at some of the reasons why we don't always love as much as we would like to, reasons which include a lack of education and support from our materialistic society and our religions to encourage us to love, even though in every area of our life there is clearly a place for love.

We established for our own satisfaction that it's completely natural for us to want to love all the time.

And finally, we began to understand that love is a very great power that we need to know how to use for the benefit of ourselves and others.

So now we have a basis on which we can feel motivated to devote some time to learn to love more. Are you loving this?

Quiz 1:

(Answers below)

Qu. 1. What would be the most loving responses you'd make in the following situations:

You're often in the company of someone who behaves hatefully towards some other person or people; what would be your most loving response to them?

1.   Tell them they are behaving hatefully and they should stop it
2.   Feel compassion towards them and stay out of their way
3.   Agree with them so as to keep their friendship sweet

Qu. 2: A person begging in the street asks you for some money; do you

1.   Suggest to them where they can go to receive State assistance
2.   Ignore them, to encourage them to be more self-responsible
3.   Give them some money and thank them for asking you

Qu. 3: The driver in front of you does something really careless or inconsiderate; do you think:

1.   "You should have your license taken away"
2.   "I love you"
3.   I don't think anything; I don't judge people.

Preferred answers:

Qu. 1: 2
Qu. 2: 3
Qu. 3: 2

———————————————————

4. WHAT IS LOVE?

Lecture 1: Section Introduction

In this section we're going to look at definitions of love, and get a better idea of what love is.

"My love is like a red, red rose, that's newly sprung in June", as the Scots poet Robert Burns sang, long ago, and Prince Charles is fond of reciting today; but this isn't quite going to cut it for our purposes here, though we might like love always to be romantic like that.

Here's a link to Prince Charles' recitation of Burns' poem, though I can't guarantee the link is still active.

https://www.bbc.co.uk/arts/robertburns/works/my_luve_is_-like_a_red_red_rose/

Let's look at some dictionary definitions, and then put a few of these definitions under a closer look, and see if we can't develop a clearer understanding and feeling for what we're talking about when we say "I'm learning to love more".

Lecture 2: Definitions Of Love

Google defines 'love', as a noun, as "a strong feeling of affection", as in fondness, tenderness, warmth, intimacy, attachment, endearment, devotion, adoration, idolization, worship, passion, desire, lust, yearning, infatuation, adulation.

It also defines 'love', as a noun, as "a great interest and pleasure in something", as in "his love for football", a liking, a weakness, partiality, leaning, proclivity, inclination, disposition.

And then 'love' as a verb, "to feel deep affection or sexual love for someone", as in being in love with, be infatuated with, be besotted with, be passionate about.

A dictionary, The Urban Dictionary, describes "Love" as nature's way of tricking people into reproducing, which is probably true but I think it must be The Urban Dictionary's little joke.

However, it goes on to say that love is, "The most spectacular, indescribable, deep euphoric feeling for someone. Love is an incredibly powerful word, when you're in love, you always want to be together, and when you're not, you're thinking about being together because you need that person and without them your life is incomplete.

"This love is unconditional affection with no limits or conditions: completely loving someone. It's when you trust the other with your life and when you would do anything for each other. When you love someone you want nothing more than for them to be truly happy no matter what it takes because that's how much you care about them and because their needs come before your own. You hide nothing of yourself and can tell the other anything because you know they accept you just the way you are and vice versa."

Okay, that kind of love, wonderful though it is, and I could encourage you in that, is only being experienced in the one-to-one relationship between two people. I want to extend this beyond the one-to-one relationship, because I'm asking you to learn to love more, not just in the sense of the depth of your love for one person, but your love's length and breadth too, that is, how you can deeply love everyone and everything, and the whole world even.

So let's look at some quotations from people who we might describe as masters, male and female.

The Greek philosopher Sophocles said "One word frees us from all the weight and pain of life: that word is love."

Actually the WikiHow website says that the Greeks broke "Love" down into four categories; one is agape, or unconditional love, as in "God loves us with all our faults."; another is our likings or needs and desires, as in "I love going for a walk"; another is family love, and the nonsexual love between close friends, as in a very deep feeling of attachment, often with physical contact such as hugs and kisses; actually, hugging and kissing was said in a study published in the *Journal of Social Psychological and Personality Science* in 2012 to be the top reason for nearly half of all men and women in a representative sample of 274 married couples saying they were still "very intensely in love" with their partner even after 10 years of marriage; and the fourth of the Greeks' definitions is the sexual love, or eroticism. Somehow, making love for reproduction doesn't seem to figure in the Greeks' reckonings.

www.wikihow.com/Define-Love

Psychologists, apparently, break love down into three components; one is physical desire, one is emotional closeness, connectedness and warmth of friendship; the third is commitment, as in, "is this a couple willing to work things out?"

The English poet Elizabeth Barrett Browning, in the 19th century wrote in a poem she called, "How do I love thee?": How do I love thee? Let me count the ways. I love thee to the depth and breadth and height my soul can reach, when feeling out of sight."

I like that one. I'll come back to that one later.

But Shakespeare warns that "Love is not love which alters when it alteration finds"; so if you fall out of love for some reason, it wasn't really love in the first place.

Okay. I think we might get the feeling that those definitions are talking mostly about romantic love. Some of them suggested more than that, such as Google, with 'worship', perhaps of God, and love of family and friends.

I'm looking for two things: how *our* love, not just the love of God, can be universal, infinite and unconditional, and how we can experience love as a powerful law of nature in our own hands which can make very good things happen, not just in your own life, in your own relationships, whether family, friends, work colleagues, strangers in the street, but also in the wider world.

As Mahatma Gandhi said, "There is a force in the universe, which, if we permit it, will flow through us and produce miraculous results."

I believe that force to be love. And in this course we'll be looking at where it is, how to access it, and how it may produce miraculous results.

But first of all, in the next lecture(s) I want to continue looking at definitions of love, by looking at the qualities, or attributes, or aspects of love through which we express and experience love in our everyday life.

Lecture 3: Aspects of Love

Usually we find ourselves expressing love in a variety of ways that we might not immediately think of as expressions of love. But they are. As Elizabeth Barrett Browning wrote, "Let me count the ways."

Here are over 30 ways; I'm sure you could think of more, and I've added a Worksheet to the resources section of this lecture so that you can add some more when you think of them, or more definitions of the ones I'm describing now:

Appreciation:

Appreciation is when you genuinely, sincerely see the virtue in someone or something. There is a glowing quality about appreciation which comes from the heart, and also from the mind because you've thought about what it is you're appreciating; but in the glow from the heart is the glow of love.

Compassion:

Compassion is the feeling you get when your heart goes out to someone in their particular circumstances. Someone whom you feel you would love to help evokes the feeling of compassion. You may feel moved to do something about it, for instance, donate towards the relief of victims of a natural disaster. Sometimes you can't do as much as you would like to do, and you are left with your heart extended towards the other person or people. Compassion (literally: with passion) is love which connects you to another but which remains unfulfilled until that time when fulfillment comes.

Gratitude:

Gratitude is the sense of thankfulness and joy that comes from receiving, whether you are actually receiving from someone or you are joyful that you are able to give. Gratitude is heartfelt love that has no bounds and is unconditional once the reason for gratitude is recognized. One may feel grateful to be alive, for no reason other than one recognizes that one is alive; or because it's a beautiful day; or because one has survived an accident or disaster or threatening situation. Whichever is the case, one draws upon that aspect of love which is gratitude, thankfulness without measure, unconditionally.

Forgiveness/Forgetfulness:

If you forgive someone who hurt you, it's an act of love towards them, whether they know you're forgiving them or not. They may not acknowledge that they hurt you; the point is, you need to relieve yourself from that hurt. So forgiving someone is an act of love towards yourself also.

If you forgive yourself for hurting someone, it's an act of love towards yourself, acknowledging your guilt, learning your lesson and relieving yourself of the debilitating guilt which serves no-one's good purpose.

In both cases, your forgiveness and forgetfulness is an act of love.

Kindness:

Kindness is one of the active forms of love; to be a kind person, or to have kindliness, implies that an action will be taken, or has the potential to be taken, which is beneficial to, considerate of, supportive of, another person. Kindness, or kindliness, suggests that a person holds it in their heart always to be kind. It is an aspect of love which is cultivated over time and has a quality of permanence and unconditionality, ever ready to be offered to someone in need.

Nurturing/Care:

Nurturing and care are aspects of love which are given to support a process, most usually of growth or sustenance, whether it be for a person, a child for example in its growth, or someone who is vulnerable in some way; or it may be for a community or other kind of group; or even a project of some sort which is being developed. In every case a quality of support is being given which draws deeply on the carer's heartfelt love, beyond a merely practical schedule of actions calculated to be of appropriate support.

Unity/Oneness/Togetherness/Belonging/Cohesion:

The sense of togetherness or belonging comes from the sense of being part of something, a family, a community, a workforce, a faith, a nationality, a race of people, etc., and if that sense of togetherness is strong, and is valued, it is felt as an aspect of love. We tend to want this sense of togetherness, we may long for it if it is absent. We like to feel that our togetherness is strong, the stronger the better. We like to feel that our sense of togetherness is love. We might wish to love the whole world if we could get over the barriers we erect to keep us separated.

Empathy:

Empathy is the sense that we have become, or could become, at one with another, sufficiently to experience the other's life as they do.

This requires a willingness to enter into the other's heart and mind; it requires the ability to put aside one's own experiences and to surrender oneself to the experiences of the other. Empathy is a gift of love, laying down one's own experiences for another's; being willing to enter into the other's experiences to an extremely high degree; and being able and willing to offer the other appropriate validation and support.

Charity:

To give in charity, whether one gives in service or in kind, is to give from the heart in an act of love. When one gives in charity, one doesn't seek anything in return, not even the satisfaction of giving; otherwise one is merely trading. Charity is the heart being extended to another in their time of need. Love seeks always to give from itself; charity is its way.

Beauty:

Beauty is the highest experience of love in the outer world. Beauty is experienced as a reflection of the highest conception of love made manifest in the outer world. This does not need to be a physical object; beauty can be experienced within a process of some sort, for example in the quality of relationships between people or animals etc. Beauty can be enduring or ephemeral; in the case of people there may be outer beauty or inner beauty; the beauty is exclusively the experience of the beholder, as a projected reflection of the beauty intrinsic within the love which we are.

Trust/Surrender/Innocence:

Trust is the surrendering of oneself to a person or process, physical or spiritual. Trust is the confidence that all will be well. Trust may be based upon an intellectual analysis of a person or process, but the giving of trust is heart-based. One feels that one can trust; in the final analysis one's heart tells one that trust is appropriate; the heart's doors innocently open and trust is given. Trust is given as an expression of love for the other.

Honesty/Openness/Sharing/Vulnerability:

The ability to give freely of oneself is an act of love. To expose oneself totally to another is the highest expression of giving from oneself unconditionally. To be honest and open and share with another
or with others, is to surrender oneself to another; one may hope that
this will be respected appropriately by the other, and any doubts that
one may have about the appropriateness of sharing so honestly is a
reflection of how profound a gift of love your honesty is.

Gentleness/Gentility/Courtesy/ Consideration/Respect:

To be gentle, to be courteous and respectful is to display the finer
qualities of love; one expects and assumes that it is always appropriate to display the finer qualities of love; we adopt these qualities in
any of our relationships in which we seek to engender a mutually
agreeable balance, whatever the circumstances may be. Gentleness is
an unmistakable indication that we are considerate of the other, and
an open door to mutual gentility.

Happiness/Fulfillment:

Happiness is a sure sign that love is being fulfilled. Happiness is felt
in the heart when sufficient fulfillment of love's desire is experienced
that the doors to the heart can open and reveal the warmth of your
love. Happiness is that aspect of love that confirms that love is experiencing itself, whether for some particular reason or for none at all
other than being able to express itself unconditionally.

Grace/Beneficence/Generosity/Abundance:

Life is abundant and gives itself through love. Love is that aspect of
life that expresses the fullness of life in all its aspects. The infinite
beneficence of life is showered upon the earth through love, fulfilled
within itself and fulfilled within its giving. We too are the givers of
grace, beneficence and abundance through the generosity of our
love. We too are the givers of grace when we express the universal,
infinite and unconditional love that we are.

Freedom/Non-Controlling:

The love within us is the giver of freedom for ourselves and for others. The love within us gives us self-sufficiency in our ability to live a life of fulfillment without needing to control others. The love within us therefore frees everyone else from our needs, and therefore we seek not to control them in any way. We are not dependent upon others; we are inter-dependent with others only to the extent that we interact with them in the process of mutually collaborative living, within which all are free as a realization of our love for one another.

Humility/Humbleness:

Love is the essence of humility and humbleness; Love does not need to puff itself up with pride; it knows itself to be the greatest power imaginable; its natural state within you is therefore the state of humility and humbleness, a power whose potential is present though inactive, as the archer holds the potential of his bow drawn back before releasing.

Power/Creativity/Intelligence/Motivation/Organizing Power:

Love has the power to orchestrate the whole of life. Love is creative and it is the motive power of life just as it is in your life ("As Above, So Below"). Love is the most powerful force in the universe and the most powerful organizing force at your disposal in your own life. Love will guide you aright when all else fails you. It is, literally, all you need.

Resources:

We've looked at descriptions of more than 40 aspects of love.

There are many more, so for this exercise, you're invited to think of more aspects, and write descriptions for each of them.

For example, how about:

Peacefulness

Confidence

Acknowledgment

Release

and more....

The exercise for this part of the course is for you to write down the aspects and descriptions you come up with; and through doing that, become more aware of such expressions of love that you see in your everyday life.

____

5. THE SOURCE AND COURSE OF LOVE

Lecture 1: Section Introduction

The purpose of this section is to discuss where love is within us. What part of ourselves is that which loves? Do we love from the level of our surface self, from our personality, or do we love from somewhere deeper within ourselves?

In this section I'll explore with you the surface and the depth of ourselves, and suggest to you that the very depths of yourself are deeper than you might think, more accessible than you might think, and you have a whole lot of love to explore.

Let's begin by taking a dip into the depths of ourselves and look at where we might find love within.

Lecture 2: Universal, infinite and unconditional love

We need to start looking at the whole of life and locating ourselves within it.

We are part of life, obviously we're part of life because we're alive, and in some way directly connected to the whole of life.

Where do we find ourselves in life, how are we related to it, and where do we find love in life?

There are people who say that love is the greatest force in the universe. They say that love comes from the very source of life. How can we understand that, other than in religious, or spiritual terms? How can we understand it in scientific terms? And if we can understand that love comes from the very source of life, at which point do we ourselves connect with that love?

Let's first of all look at the idea that love comes from the source of life and the whole of life is therefore somehow imbued with love through and through.

If love comes from the source of life, how do we see it expressed in the physical universe? What would we look for, that we might describe as expressions of love?

What can we say is a fair definition of love? As the great scientist Albert Einstein said, "How are you ever going to explain in terms of chemistry and physics so important a biological phenomenon as first love?" We're not concerned with first love here, but we could also ask how can you explain love in such scientific terms?

Let's look at some of the expressions which we ourselves use when we're describing love experiences:

I am magnetically attracted to her, or him.

It felt like there was an electrical charge between us.

We gravitated towards each other across the room.

My love for her was infinite.

I care about her so much I would die for her.

We nurture our children lovingly to help them to grow.

This love gives me a stability in my life, and a purpose for being alive.

United forever are we, in purpose and being, in the eternity of love.

We're married because we wanted children. We felt marriage was important to give the children a meaningful, solid, stable framework for their lives.

I wanted children in order to continue the thread of the family lineage.

Our family holds together through thick and thin.

Can you see in these expressions principles which appear to apply throughout the universe?

The universe is full of electricity, magnetism and gravity. It is continuously creating; it is nurturing, sustaining and also allowing things to die, and be recycled. These things together, creating maintaining and destroying, are clearly part of life as an intelligent, evolving, purposeful process.

This process of creation could easily be seen as being directed by a loving hand, heart and mind, though I'm not suggesting that the universe is the work of a human-like being. I am merely suggesting that the principles underlying the process of creation are similar, very similar, to what we would describe as love, or that which holds the whole process together is what we could describe as love. This is not to say that that universal kind of love has a heartfelt quality to it. It may have no quality to it; it may be simply a force, an energy, a law of nature; but it serves to direct the process of creation, to uphold it, nurture it, support it and hold it all together in one cohesive whole; like we, in our human condition, would expect love to do.

On the other hand we may indeed have a loving God above us, in the way some religions teach. Indeed one might imagine that what is called the Holy Trinity was founded in love, and is held together by love.

One of the resources attached to this lecture is a link to a website written in the form of a book with chapters, by people who understand the principles of what is called sacred geometry, that is, the mathematical principles on which the universe was created. The website makes for very heavy reading but it's fascinating and very illuminating in the respect that the universe is shown to be imbued through and through with love. I'm very familiar with that website because I did proof-reading for it for a few years while it was in the making.

One of the things it says is "Love is the one force which is universally the same for all life regardless of frequency and involvement. Love is the single most powerful vibration in all of creation." By that reckoning we should be feeling some of that love for ourselves. I can assure you on the basis of my own, repeated experience that this is possible, without the use of mushrooms or other mind-altering substances or self-induced, so-called "peak" experiences. One can feel totally blissed-out with love, feeling self-sufficient in love and loving everyone and everything. Whether I can get you to experience that depends on how deeply you're prepared to engage yourself in this course and beyond it.

If we believe that there must be some purpose behind the creation of the universe, otherwise the whole of life would be meaningless, we can infer, and that book goes into detail over it, that the universe was created by someone or something in order to extend its existence into a new state of being. To judge from what we now know of the universe, it's possible for us to say that there was an inconceivably immense intelligence behind the intention to give birth to the universe, though not everyone's going to agree with that. There is undeniable orderliness in the physical universe even though there also appears to be chaos and destruction. But when we think of the process of re-decorating a room in our house, we see that chaos is part of the creative process; and that destruction is needed for recycling, whilst the wonderful, finished result doesn't appear until all the chaos and all the destruction is done.

Nature, as we can see it, has inconceivable intelligence. The deeper into nature our technology allows us to see, the more incredible we see the intelligence within it to be, far, far beyond what we can envisage being able to create, except perhaps for little bits at a time.

We might also say that the love behind the creation of the physical universe is unconditional, in the sense that the physical creation is apparently left to evolve as it will, having been given a very good start in life, and plenty of energy to see it through. It would be worth giving some more thought to that.

So can we establish that love is part of life, from its source to every part of the physical universe, which includes ourselves. And we can say, without far too much of a stretch, that love is universal, infinite and unconditional?

Also can we say that we ourselves, as part of the physical universe, are directly connected to that universal, infinite and unconditional love. We need only find how to access it. And I, together with some people I'm going to quote from, can show you how to do that.

I know it's pretty big "ask" to ask you to accept such a profound concept of that universal, infinite and unconditional love, and I need to ask you to stay with me on this. Believe me, I've been there, done that and got the T-shirt. It has taken me decades to gain the knowledge and experience to discuss these things authentically. I can offer you plenty of resources to enable you to delve deeply into this knowledge and gain these experiences for yourself. However I believe I can also offer you shortcuts to what I believe you really need to know. You won't have to spend the years I've spent in gaining this knowledge and experience. You just need to trust me and see this course through.

Let's go on now and look at how you can connect yourself to the whole of life.

Lecture 3: Who Are You, Really? Part 1

Who are you? Who are you, *really*?

I'm not asking what is your name. I'm not asking whether you're a father or mother, son or daughter, I'm not asking you to identify yourself by your career for example, whether you're an accountant, a gardener or hairdresser, school teacher, nurse, I don't want to know whether you're a man or a woman, what your faith is, what race you're from, what your sexuality is, I don't want any of the usual labels we give ourselves.

What are you beyond all of those labels? You might say, "I am a human being"; well your body is of the human kind, the human template. But what are you within that body? What is it that says "I am"?

When you have the thought in your mind, "I am", you might use your brain, your nervous system and your vocal mechanisms to say "I am". But where is your mind?

And what is behind your mind? Is the real you to be found in your mind or somewhere behind or beyond your mind?

Scientists have been very slow to study consciousness. They're discovering that consciousness is difficult to locate, though they are seeing that consciousness activates parts of the brain, the nervous system and the body.

I've added some scientific articles about this to the Resources section of this lecture, but I suggest that you leave them until later. What they show is that mainstream science has not yet connected the physical world with consciousness; they have not yet proven the existence of the soul; they have not identified love as a law of nature; they are however going deeper and deeper into the nature of things, and are making serious efforts to understand what people describe as the spiritual dimension of life.

There are, however, some scientists outside the academic mainstream, who have gone all the way and now fully understand what consciousness is, where it is located, and how it works. I've added some links to articles and papers about this in the resources section; but again, I suggest you leave those until later.

And in the meantime, without any scientific validation of this, let's see what we ourselves can understand about who we really are.

What is this consciousness that is aware that "I am"?

Is this the part of our self which is called spiritual?

Can we see anything in life which suggests there is a spiritual part of life?

If we were to look at a schematic showing the hierarchical nature of physical existence, or indeed of mathematics, philosophy or even computer science, we would see a common structure, at the base of which there appears to be a non-physical structure we might call spiritual. It appears that this is where the laws of nature, the intelligence of nature and the energy of life have their source.

To explain briefly, at the top of the hierarchy there is the outward expression, for example in physics we see the physical object. I'm showing this on a chart in the Resources section of this lecture.

As we proceed down the hierarchy the gross, physical expression becomes more subtle, and we begin to see the intelligence and the energy of which all things are seen to be comprised.

At the foot of the hierarchy we find the most subtle expressions, for example in physics we find electromagnetism and gravity and some sub-nuclear forces; and beneath those we move into a nonphysical field of existence in which there appears to be nothing; but clearly this is where we see the source of the outward expression. This area on the chart is sometimes called the transcendental field of existence. Or the unified field of natural law. We might also call this the spiritual dimension of existence. It is where the laws of nature originate. It is where the life beyond the physical exists.

This is where our consciousness exists, beyond our gross physical body. Within this transcendental field our individual consciousness is located and has its source. And, as it is outside the range of the physical body there is reason to believe that our consciousness may be existing independently of the body, eternally, before and after the existence of the physical body - just as the religions have been asking us to believe. If there is but one thing that we can thank the religions for it is that they have perpetuated the belief that there is a spiritual, greater dimension to our lives.

You are probably familiar with the idea that you have a spiritual soul. Here, in the transcendental field, is where your soul would be located, as is your consciousness. Your spiritual soul and your eternal consciousness can be seen to be the same. Therefore you do not have a soul, you *are* a soul. Here today in this body you are a soul. You *have* a body. You are not your body. You are your soul. You are a soul. When you say "I am" you could say, "I am a soul. I am a spiritual soul." And as that spiritual soul, you are deeply immersed in, and part of, the wholeness of life itself. You have an immediate and total connection to the whole of life itself, being part of it.

Our thoughts come from our consciousness, our soul; this is where our intuition comes from, this is where your sense of connectedness to life comes from. This is where your deeper love comes from. And the part of the body that has the connection to the soul is not the brain but the heart. The electromagnetic field surrounding the heart, connecting with the electromagnetic field outside of and around us is far greater than that surrounding the brain.

So the question now would be, how do you live as a soul? How do you access and make use of the intelligence and energy of life itself? How do you access and express the love of life itself?

We need first of all to look at how we presently live on the surface of life, in everyday life. Do we live as a soul connected to the whole of life, or do we live as a body, separate from everyone and everything? Let's look at that in the next lecture.

I'd like to say a few words about my own experiences in this. I'll do this in the next lecture.

On the next page are some resources of a theoretical nature. They're here because it's the logical place to put them. However, as I've said earlier, I suggest you skip over these and return to them later when I've given you a more practical understanding and experience of what the theories are seeking to explain without that practical understanding and experience.

Resources for Section 5, Lecture 2:

1.   The Structure of Life, As Seen Through Physics
(very, very simplified! And the most fundamental levels are not yet
fully understood by mainstream science)

Solid Object	Piece of Wood
Molecular Physics	Molecules containing atoms of carbon (approx. 50% of a piece of wood is carbon)
Atomic Physics	Atoms of carbon contain empty space where 6 tiny electrons whirl around a nucleus which, relative to the size of the whole atom, is about the size of a pea in the middle of a football pitch!)
Nuclear Physics	The nucleus of the Carbon atom has 6 protons and 6 neutrons
Quantum Physics	Protons and neutrons contain quarks, making up about 1% of protons' mass, the rest is energy holding it together
Fundamental Forces of nature	Electromagnetism, Gravity, Strong and Weak interactions, Higgs Field The breaking (how?/why?/not understood by science) of symmetry in these forces creates matter particles
Unified Field Theory	Non-physical Unified Field/Transcendental Field/Consciousness (not understood by mainstream science, but this is the source of the fundamental forces and the Laws of Nature)
Absolute Pure Being	Existence, Source of Creative Intelligence, Energy (not acknowledged by mainstream science)

2. Mainstream science does not understand consciousness: Journal articles:

Will We Ever Understand Consciousness? Scientists & Philosophers Debate

The nature of consciousness has intrigued philosophers and scientists for thousands of years. But can modern neuroscience ever hope to crack this mysterious phenomenon? At the World Science Festival, an annual celebration and exploration of science held in New York, a panel of experts debated what scientists can and can't learn about the mind by studying the brain.

Plenty of great minds have pondered the meaning of consciousness over the ages, said philosopher Colin McGinn of the University of Miami. The 17th-century French mathematician and philosopher René Descartes famously introduced the notion of mind-body dualism, which holds that the world of the body is fundamentally separate from the world of the mind, or soul, although the two may interact. In the 19th century, the English biologist Thomas Huxley helped develop the theory of epiphenomenalism, the idea that physical events in the brain give rise to mental phenomena. On the panel, McGinn also talked about panpsychism, the view that the universe is made of minds.

McGinn himself believes that no matter how much scientists study the brain, the mind is fundamentally incapable of comprehending itself. "We're rather like Neanderthals trying to understand astronomy or Shakespeare" McGinn said. Human brains suffer from a "cognitive gap" in understanding their own consciousness, he said.

Read more at: https://www.livescience.com/what-is-consciousness-mystery.html

Scientists Closing in on Theory of Consciousness

https://www.livescience.com/does-consciousness-pervade-the-universe.html

Probably for as long as humans have been able to grasp the concept of consciousness, they have sought to understand the phenomenon.

Studying the mind was once the province of philosophers, some of whom still believe the subject is inherently unknowable. But neuroscientists are making strides in developing a true science of the self.

Here are some of the best contenders for a theory of consciousness:

Read more at: https://www.livescience.com/does-consciousness-pervade-the-universe.html

Hard problem of consciousness

https://en.wikipedia.org/wiki/Hard_problem_of_consciousness

Several questions about consciousness must be resolved in order to acquire a full understanding of it. These questions include, but are not limited to, whether being conscious could be wholly described in physical terms, such as the aggregation of neural processes in the brain. If consciousness *cannot* be explained exclusively by physical events, it must transcend the capabilities of physical systems and require an explanation of nonphysical means. For philosophers who assert that consciousness is nonphysical in nature, there remains a question about what outside of physical theory is required to explain consciousness.

Why can't the world's greatest minds solve the problem of consciousness?

https://www.theguardian.com/news/audio/2015/jan/30/podcast-consciousness-burkeman-audio

"It is remarkable," they began, "that most of the work in both cognitive science and the neurosciences makes no reference to consciousness" – partly, they suspected, "because most workers in these areas cannot see any useful way of approaching the problem". They presented their own "sketch of a theory", arguing that certain neurons, firing at certain frequencies, might somehow be the cause of our inner awareness – though it was not clear how.

Hear more at: https://www.theguardian.com/news/audio/2015/jan/30/podcast-consciousness-burkeman-audio

3. SOME modern science has an understanding of consciousness

Note from your course instructor:

A major intention with this course is to introduce students to the most modern and advanced level of scientific thinking in relation to love; particularly, to an understanding that love can be understood in scientific terms, notably through the scientific, theoretical and practical study of human consciousness, as I have studied and experienced.

In the past, we have (or have not) accepted religious teachings as the basis for the fundamental truth of our lives; more recently, we have sought truth from mainstream science as the greatest authority on "reality". Largely, we still do depend on mainstream science in this way.

However, since the 1920s, science has been exploring a more fundamental understanding of reality through quantum physics, or quantum mechanics, which has proved to be a seemingly infinitely rich source of information, though mind-bogglingly difficult to fathom in its entirety.

Nonetheless, quantum mechanics is providing us with a wholly new understanding of the reality of our lives, and it makes our previous understandings, based on the Newtonian, mechanistic model of our physical reality, hopelessly inadequate; and the religious teachings even more dependent on faith alone for our understanding of the spiritual dimensions of life. The religions really ought now to be teaching the fundamentals of quantum mechanics as a way to authenticate the truths of their age-old spiritual teachings, as quantum mechanics and unified field theory can now begin to do.

Here is a selection of scientists who have studied quantum mechanics and begun to develop a better understanding of the connections between human consciousness and the greater reality in which we live; some have gone so far as to state that love is the ultimate truth, the bottom line, the answer to everything, and that we can connect with that love on its cosmic scale — which is what this course is showing students how to do.

John Hagelin: Is Consciousness the Unified Field?

https://www.scienceandnonduality.com/videos/john-hagelin-is-consciousness-the-unified-field/

Progress in theoretical physics during the past decade has led to a progressively more unified understanding of the laws of nature, culminating in the recent discovery of complete unified field theories based on the superstring. These theories identify a single universal, unified field at the basis of all forms and phenomena in the universe.

At the same time, cutting-edge research in the field of neuroscience has revealed the existence of a 'unified field of consciousness'—a fourth major state of human consciousness, which is physiologically and subjectively distinct from waking, dreaming and deep sleep. In this meditative state, a.k.a. Samadhi, the threefold structure of waking experience—the observer, the observed and the process of observation—are united in one indivisible wholeness of pure consciousness.

Read more at: https://www.scienceandnonduality.com/videos/john-hagelin-is- consciousness-the-unified-field/

Unified field of consciousness from the perspective of QUANTUM PHYSICS

https://tmhome.com/benefits/unified-field-of-consciousness-onemany/

What sounds radically new in the field of neuroscience has been a familiar paradigm in modern physics. The seeds of the theory were laid already by Albert Einstein himself when he postulated that everything in the universe is relative and the existence of different worlds and forms and phenomena can only be accounted for in terms of relativity.

One of the first physicists to take this perspective to its logical and scientific conclusion was David Bohm. The founding father of quantum physics proposed several metaphors for what the reality of energy/matter continuum looked like.

Read more at: https://tmhome.com/benefits/unified-field-of-consciousness-onemany/

Quantum Particles, Consciousness, Unified Field Theory And Relativity

https://www.academia.edu/7001927/Quantum_Particles_Consciousness_Unified _Field_Theory_And_Relativity

It is evident that consciousness is the central player in the scheme of things in nature.

Thus, even if a unified field theory or theory of everything were obtained, it will still not give a complete picture of nature if consciousness were excluded. There should therefore be a complementary General Theory of Consciousness. This General Theory of Consciousness will be a very important aspect in our search for the ultimate truth. Many scientists, e.g. David Bohm, Wolfgang Pauli, John von Neumann, Arthur Eddington, Roger Penrose, George Wald, etc., had declared that the universe is mind-stuff.

Read more at:

https://www.academia.edu/7001927/Quantum_Particles_Consciousness_Unified _Field_Theory_And_Relativity

Quantum Theory Proves That Consciousness Moves to Another Universe After Death

https://www.learning-mind.com/quantum-theory-proves-that-consciousness-moves-to-another-universe-after-death/

Professor Stuart Hameroff from the University of Arizona has no doubts about the existence of eternal soul. Last year, he announced that he has found evidence that consciousness does not perish after death. According to Hameroff, the human brain is the perfect quantum computer, and the soul, or consciousness, is simply information stored at the quantum level. It can be transferred, following the death of the body; quantum information carried by consciousness merges with our universe and exists infinitely. In his turn, Lanza proves that the soul migrates to another universe. That is the main difference his theory has from the similar ones.

Read more at: https://www.learning-mind.com/quantum-theory-proves-that- consciousness-moves-to-another-universe-after-death/

Thomas Campbell, Quantum Physicist and Consciousness Researcher: Consciousness The Ultimate Reality

https://www.youtube.com/watch?v=0AihD2__gKE

Thomas Campbell was interviewed together with Bruce Lipton, who is a stem cell biologist and internationally recognized leader in bridging science and spirit. This 2hr interview gives a fascinating insight and confirmation that the fundamental element in both biology and physics (and by inference, all sciences) is love:

Bruce Lipton and Tom Campbell – Part ONE

https://www.youtube.com/watch?v=FWUu9BTi3X8 (important note: before watching, reduce the volume of the very beginning, introductory sounds are much too loud)

Bruce Lipton and Tom Campbell – Part TWO

https://www.youtube.com/watch?v=As-nPkjQJZg

Lecture 3: Going Deeper

Back in the 1980s, I practiced Transcendental Meditation, or TM as it's often called.

I'm not going to suggest that you practice TM because it requires something of a change of lifestyle, not to mention costing quite a bit to learn these days. Also I think I can offer you some of the understandings I gained from practicing TM without you having to learn and practice it yourself.

I learned to practice TM because I was told that it would help me fulfill my own potential. In fact shortly after learning the basic practice of TM I went on to learn and practice an advanced form of TM, now popularly known as Yogic Flying. I'm adding some resources to this lecture to show you something of what I'm talking about.

The whole idea of TM is to transcend, or go deeper than, or go beyond, the ordinary, waking state of the mind and settle the mind into the transcendental field of consciousness which is a very quiet state of mind. In that state of mind, the body can release stress effectively, thus improving health, mood and overall well-being. More importantly, it enables one to get in touch with one's deeper, and deepest state of being, absolute pure being, which is a state of deep silence and deep rest. And it gives you the idea that your consciousness is more than you'd known it to be.

The yogic flying program, taking this further, enables one to engage in action from that deep state of being. Doing so, one is drawing from a very powerful field of being, and stirring the laws of nature themselves.

TM teaches that there is a single field of consciousness, a field of creative intelligence, of which our individual consciousness is part, and that when we are meditating we are having a beneficial effect not just on ourselves but also on other people too. It is reckoned that if 1% of a population were meditating, it would have a significant, beneficial effect on the quality of life for the entire population.

With the more powerful yogic flying technique, when practiced as a group, only the *square root* of 1% of a population is needed to benefit the entire population's quality of life. So in the case of Britain where I was practicing yogic flying, a group of only 800 people would suffice to improve the quality of life of the whole nation, somewhere near 64 million population.

In scientific terms, yogic flying was reckoned to be the equivalent of laser light by comparison with the light from an ordinary lightbulb.

When we were practicing yogic flying in large groups, when we were able to achieve a high degree of group unity by virtue of all of us being in the transcendental field at the same time, statistical research was carried out which proved that our yogic flying had pronounced benefits for the whole of Britain; or for Europe when we were joining yogic flyers from around Europe.

I tell you this to show you that I have practical experience of the benefits of accessing the power of the transcendental field of consciousness, which I am asking you to access, though without you having to practice the transcendental meditation. You will be able to access the power of the transcendental field of consciousness simply by recognizing that that is where your own consciousness is located; identifying yourself as that consciousness, and recognizing that you have access to the whole of that field of consciousness which is infinite, creative and very powerful. To understand that better, you could begin to relate it, just vaguely at this stage, to what some of the religions talk about as the spiritual dimension of life.

You will be able to access more of that power, albeit not on the same scale, when you have a degree of unity with another person, or with a group of people, as we were with our yogic flying, but we'll come to how you can do that later.

Resources:

Yogic Flying – some info

https://www.youtube.com/watch?v=NHwhGUo9Cjw

https://www.permanentpeace.org/technology/yogic_flying.html

http://www.amazingabilities.com/amaze9a.html

https://www.tm.org/meditation-techniques

Lecture 4: How To Go Deeper Into Life And Love

If you're going to access and utilize the greater dimension of love in your life, there are six main things for you to do.

Firstly, you must recognize that you are an embodiment of love, a spiritual soul and you are seated in the spiritual dimension of life now, here, today, tomorrow and always.

Secondly, you must *be* who you really are; you must identify yourself as a soul, and realize and actualize yourself as a soul in your everyday life in order to draw on the universal, infinite and unconditional love that you have at your disposal because that's what you are.

Thirdly, you must get a better idea of what your purpose in life is; what does your life suggest your purpose is? Have you ever thought your life might have a particular purpose? What have you ever thought your purpose might be? To what extent are you already living it? How could you add more of your purpose to your life?

It's quite possible that you're already living your purpose to quite some degree. As I said earlier, I believe that the subconscious or unconscious part of our mind is more active than we realize, and it may have been steering us in the right direction all our life.

Fourthly, you must reorientate your life to that purpose as fully as you can, in order to align yourself most productively to the universal, infinite and unconditional love, and to its creative intelligence and organizing power, that you have at your disposal.

Fifthly, you must be an embodiment of love in action, towards yourself, towards your family and friends, to strangers on the street, to workmates, members of groups you're in, your neighbors and community, and to the wider world, to whatever extent is appropriate in the circumstances, and to which you're able.

Sixthly, you need to see more love in the world. The world we see out there is a reflection of the love we give to it. If we want the world to look more loving, we need to see it through more loving eyes. Then we'll see that the world is already full of love; it simply needs to be brought to your attention by virtue of you knowing it. Does all of that sound like a circular argument? That's exactly what it is. The world you see is how you see it.

In these ways you'll be able to access a deeper level of love in your life, and you'll discover more of the power that love has to transform the world around you.

Resources:

Here's a video I made in 2014 as a meditation to describe what I've just said - unconditional love is who you are.

https://youtu.be/VFsoewpTrDU

Lecture 5: Section Conclusion

What we have done in this section is to open a window into the greater dimensions of your life. We have established that there is what, for our purposes, may best be described as a spiritual dimension to our lives, a dimension where we may say our real self is located and exists, here, today and always.

The scientific study of consciousness points to this as a reality. I am adding some resources to this lecture to enable you to see some of the scientific research.

This spiritual dimension is where we are connected to the whole of life, where we have access to the whole of life, where the laws of nature have their source, where the intelligence, energy and love which life is have their source. We are therefore left to see ourselves as part of something extremely powerful, infinite as far as we can tell, and the source of universal and unconditional love.

We have established that our consciousness, what we might call our individual soul, is seated in that dimension. There is reason to believe that as a soul we are eternal and it is only our body which is temporary and will die. We are not a body which has a soul, somewhere. Rather, we are a soul, here now and always, which has a body - for now.

The soul, being eternal, has a great deal of interest in this life, your life. The soul, together with the spiritual dimensions of which it is part, is concerned with the opportunities that this physical incarnation of yours provides, whether as a source of spiritual growth, or as an opportunity for service to mankind, or the Earth, or the greater whole, in some way.

One might think that it's the ego, your outward sense of being alive and being who you are, which has the most invested in this life, because this life will be all the ego has. However, the ego is best understood to be a tool for living whatever the purpose of your life is. It is important therefore, to have a good sense of what your life is really all about.

To do this, having opened the window into the greater dimensions of our life, we need to develop an understanding of what our soul has in mind for this life and explore how to access the resources which life, in its material and spiritual dimensions, affords us. In this course we are discussing how we may learn to love more. The whole thrust of this course is that we may access the universal, infinite and unconditional love of the greater, spiritual dimension of life. It is the universal, infinite and unconditional love of the greater spiritual dimension of life that is the motive power and creative intelligence behind our life. So we need now to reorientate ourselves towards living a life of love as our real, spiritual selves here today, in this body, in this material life of ours.

Resources:

Consciousness in the spiritual dimension/unified field/transcendental field

Quantum Theory Proves That Consciousness Moves to Another Universe After Death

Read more at: https://www.learning-mind.com/quantum-theory-proves-that-consciousness-moves-to-another-universe-after-death/

A book titled "Biocentrism: How Life and Consciousness Are the Keys to Understanding the Nature of the Universe", published in the USA, has stirred up the Internet because of the notion that life does not end when the body dies and can last forever. The author of this publication, scientist Robert Lanza, has no doubts that this may be possible. Beyond time and space Lanza is an expert in regenerative medicine and scientific director at Advanced Cell Technology Company. While he is known for his extensive research on stem cells, he was also famous for several successful experiments on cloning endangered animal species. But not so long ago, the scientist turned his attention to physics, quantum mechanics and astrophysics. This explosive mixture has given birth to the new theory of biocentrism, which the professor has been preaching ever since.

Read more at: https://www.learning-mind.com/quantum-theory-proves-that-consciousness-moves-to-another-universe-after-death/

John Hagelin: Is Consciousness the Unified Field?

https://www.scienceandnonduality.com/videos/john-hagelin-is-consciousness-the-unified-field/

Progress in theoretical physics during the past decade has led to a progressively more unified understanding of the laws of nature, culminating in the recent discovery of completely unified field theories based on the superstring. These theories identify a single universal, unified field at the basis of all forms and phenomena in the universe.

At the same time, cutting-edge research in the field of neuroscience has revealed the existence of a 'unified field of consciousness'—a fourth major state of human consciousness, which is physiologically and subjectively distinct from waking, dreaming and deep sleep. In this meditative state, a.k.a. Samadhi, the threefold structure of waking experience—the observer, the observed and the process of observation—are united in one indivisible wholeness of pure consciousness.

Hear more at: https://www.scienceandnonduality.com/videos/john-hagelin-is-consciousness-the-unified-field/

Energy, Consciousness, and the Unified Field

Nassim Haramein interviewed by Dr. Paul Drouin

https://www.youtube.com/watch?v=1zjppOA7FiU

In this video, **Nassim Haramein** is interviewed by **Dr. Paul Drouin** on the principles of unified field theory, quantum gravity, consciousness studies, energy, and their far-reaching implications that unify the fields of both biology and physics.

Quantum Particles, Consciousness, Unified Field Theory And Relativity

https://www.academia.edu/7001927/Quantum_Particles_Consciousness_Unified _Field_Theory_And_Relativity

A number of scientists had postulated that there must be a "cosmic consciousness" pervading the universe.

QUIZ 2: Love is in the air?

This quiz asks where is the full potential of love to be found in your life?

(Answers below)

1.   The principle 'As Above, So Below' indicates that love is to be found in some form throughout the universe as well as in our own lives. Which historical person first identified that principle?

William Shakespeare
Albert Einstein
Mahatma Gandhi
A Greek God
Charles Darwin

2.   How would you see yourself in your efforts to be all that you were born to be?

As a rich person
As a dedicated follower of fashion
As a person in the prime of life
As a spiritual soul
As a person of high social status
However I choose to be

3.   How can you access and utilize the greater dimensions of love in your life?

Recognize that you're a spiritual soul here in your physical body
Actualize yourself as a spiritual soul living in this physical world of matter
Identify your uniqueness and your unique purpose in life, if you have one
Be an embodiment of love
See the world through the eyes of love
The first three of the above
All of the above

Answers:

Question 1:

A Greek God

The (mythical?) Greek God Hermes is said to be the first to voice the 'As Above, So Below' principle, saying "That which is above is like that which is below, and that which is below is like that which is above."

Question 2:

As a spiritual soul

As a spiritual soul you're connected with the whole of life itself, not separate from everything as your mind and body might have you believe in this physical life. As a spiritual soul, your potential is within easy reach at all times, through love.

Question 3:

All of the above

This is the best answer because all of these have their important part to play if you're to realize your full potential - which is not difficult to do.

---

6. IDENTIFICATION WITH EGO OR SOUL

Lecture 1: Section Introduction

The purpose of this lecture is to consider to what extent you live as if you are separate from everyone and everything, or connected to everyone and everything.

As we were growing up we developed an identity for ourselves, a personality, and an approach to life, all of which are distinctly our own. To do this we have developed our ego. The ego is a tool we use to develop our individuality, our personality and our front, or face, or image through which we relate to other people and through which other people will identify us and relate to us.

The question we now need to ask ourselves is: is this ego a true representation of our real selves, or have we given ourselves an identity entirely of our own design bearing little relation to our real self, our soul?

Let's see in this section.

Lecture 2: Your self-identification as an ego

You might argue that the identity, or ego, you have created for yourself enables you to be successful in your life. It enables you to achieve what you want for yourself. And this would largely be because you believe that all you have to work with is your individual, separate self, your ego.

Let's see to what extent you have developed a strong ego to help you through your life. In the resources section of this lecture you will find a worksheet questionnaire which will help you to calculate the strength of your ego. I'd appreciate it if you would go to this questionnaire now and answer the questions, add up the total and read my comments about the strength of your ego and its effectiveness in your life.

Ideally, do this before you go on to the next lecture.

Lecture 3: Your self-identification as a soul

Now let's look at the degree to which you identify yourself as a soul. This would mean that you consider yourself essentially to be a spiritual being, connected with everyone and everything, living your life as part of the whole of life, and drawing on the resources that the whole of life provides.

To whatever extent you identify yourself as a soul *and also* as a distinct, separate personality, or ego, this will determine the extent to which you are drawing on the resources of the whole of life and/or whatever resources you can accumulate for yourself from what you find around you.

As a soul you might feel that you have an immense reservoir to draw upon, and you will tend to be a giving person. You might also feel that things generally work out for you very well, without much effort. You may feel very blessed in your life.

Again, there is a worksheet questionnaire in the resources section of this lecture. I'd appreciate it if you would go to it now, answer the questions on it and add up the total. Again, you will find my comments about the extent to which you are identifying yourself as a soul.

Lecture 4: Section Conclusion

It is my belief, based on my understandings and experience, that the more we are oriented towards our soul, accessing the greater, spiritual dimensions of our life, the more we will draw upon love, and the more love we will express, give to others, and feel within ourselves. Also, in drawing on the greater, spiritual dimensions of life, we will draw upon the most positive, uplifting, constructive and holistic organizing power of life, which will be to everyone's benefit, not just our own. Hence the purpose of this course, to inspire, encourage and enable you to do that - to love more, and specifically to draw on the greater spiritual dimensions of your life for the benefits it brings to you and others.

I'd now like to go on in the next section to discuss the practical ways in which you could love more.

Resources:

Questionnaire: Your self-identification as an ego

How much are you invested in your ego?

Tick the ones that apply to you!

I am more concerned with my own interests than other people's ______

I am competitive ______

I am argumentative, forthright, combative ______

I am much affected by criticism and/or compliments ______

I am frequently fearful ______

I seek to be attractive to others ______

I hope to be impressive in the eyes of others ______

I like to 'shine' amongst company   _______

I talk more than the average amongst company   _______

I tend to be boastful   _______

I often dislike, hate and/or despise other people   _______

I often feel superior or inferior to other people   _______

I am often self-conscious and/or shy in some
situations   _______

I tend to hold grudges and/or find it hard to forgive   _______

I have a strong personality   _______

I will actively defend myself against criticism   _______

I will retaliate when negatively impacted by people   _______

I often find things don't work out well for me   _______

I sometimes take undue advantage of other people   _______

I aspire to improve my social standing/status   _______

I am ruthless in pursuit of my own interests   _______

I am materialistic and/or consumerist in my lifestyle   _______

I expect payment for work outside family and
friends   _______

I never give money to people begging on the
street   _______

My idea of 'family' is limited to blood relatives   _______

                    Total number of ticked items: _______

Ego investment analysis

Score 0 - 8:

The lower the score you have in this range, the nearer you are to having your ego in its proper place.

Your ego is a tool in the hands of your higher self, your soul. Your ego is that part of you that enables you to function in this life as an individual, as a personality, able to live in a way which is compatible with your purpose in this life. Your low score suggests you are using your ego in moderation, which is good.

Your life is not meaningless; it is not appropriate to live your life as if it's all about what you want and how you wish to live your life in a manner of your own choosing, regardless of anyone else. Your score suggests that you are already aware of that, consciously or intuitively to some extent at least.

The other side of this equation is that you will probably gain a fairly high score on the Soul-investment questionnaire. So you have your soul and your ego in their proper balance. However...

Too low a score for your ego combined with a high score for your soul may present a risk that other people may walk over you, and take undue advantage of you. You need to be able to fend people off in such circumstances, so your ego does need to have some strength to stand up for yourself.

Score 9 - 15:

Your mid-range score suggests that you recognized at a fairly early age that you are an individual who can make your life your own, and can take some responsibility for what you make yourself into. You are self-aware enough to recognize your strengths, weaknesses and feelings, and you do what you feel is necessary to protect yourself, and further yourself, in this competitive world.

This is fairly typical for someone living in the developed world. There's a lot of competition out there, and if we're going to make a success for ourselves, we have to make the most of our assets and opportunities. We may sometimes feel we don't like to be the way we are, but we can justify it in terms of being reasonably successful without hurting too many people along the way.

On the whole, you may think that you're doing okay. But the kind of life we lead in the developed world is beguiling, and it is very easy to lose sight of the higher values that might transform this world into something better for all. You might hope to make even more of a success for yourself, but it's as well to remember the saying, "For what shall it profit a man if he shall gain the whole world and lose his own soul?"

Score 16 and over:

This high score suggests that you have let your ego take over your life. It has created an identity for you according to its own design, which may bear little if any relation to who you really are.   It is most probably a fearful thing, ever conscious of the possibility of attack in the form of criticism or opposition.

The ego in every person has a transient existence, existing only for the duration of this lifetime, whereas your spiritual soul goes on forever. In your case, your over-inflated ego is desperate to survive, and yet in creating this fake identity it makes itself vulnerable to its own destruction at any moment. You're probably very offended to hear that.

You have allowed your ego to take full control. The fake strength that it appears to the outside world to have, and makes it so successful in creating a favorable impression (so it thinks), makes it very difficult for you to imagine living any other way.

When you love, if you love, your love may be a projection of your real self desperate to express itself, or it may be a fake 'love' intended to create a favorable impression of yourself, or serve some purpose of your own.

It's time to give some serious consideration to extricating yourself from the control of your ego, and learning to live as the spiritual soul that you truly are, loving from your soul, unconditionally, everyone and everything; and to remember that you, as a spiritual soul, are loved unconditionally beyond measure by the whole of life itself.

Next:

Questionnaire on your self-identification as a soul

How much are you invested in your soul?

Tick each of the items that apply to you:

I am more concerned with other people's/society's well-being than my own   ————

I allow other people to 'shine' more than me   ————

I enjoy and am energized by helping other people   ————

I contribute to charitable work   ————

I feel concerned for people in less comfortable circumstances than my own   ————

I consider 'family' extends beyond blood relatives   ————

I am comfortable working in groups   ————

I am happy that other people take the credit for group achievements   ————

I enjoy witnessing other people's successes   ————

I am considerate/compassionate/empathetic towards other people   ————

I do things for people without asking to be repaid   ————

I derive pleasure from simple acts of kindness   ————

I engage in 'saving the world' in some way   ————

I believe that there is a higher or spiritual dimension to my life   ————

I live mindfully of my impact on my spiritual life   ————

I often listen to my intuition/inner voice/conscience   ————

I experience fortunate synchronicities/coincidences/luck quite often   ————

I feel connected to other people, to nature, to life

I believe there are higher spiritual beings or powers

I strive to live in accord with those higher spiritual beings or powers

I strive to live mindfully of my soul, or to be my soul

I believe there is a higher creative, organizing intelligence of some sort

I strive to live in alignment with that higher creative,
organizing intelligence

I believe that love can be unconditional for everyone
and everything

I do, at least sometimes, feel unconditional love for
everyone and everything

I see others as souls rather than their physical bodies
and personalities

I believe my consciousness will survive the death of my
body

I believe in 'out of body' experiences, 'I went to Heav-
en' near-death experiences

Total number of ticked items   _______

Soul Investment Analysis

Score 0 - 10:

Even a low score suggests that you are living the values of your higher self, your soul. Unless you are living such higher values as consideration, concern, care and compassion, etc for the benefit of your ego, and the rewards they will bring to you, you are holding a good balance between your ego and your soul, which is necessary for you to live rightfully in this challenging world.

As such, with this good balance, you are probably leading a good life, respected and valued by those who know you. You have a positive personality and disposition, ready to play your part as a member of the groups you live, work and play with. You probably have some confidence that you are living your life aright, which you most probably are.

Knowing, as you do, the value of the higher values of life, you may wish to see such values prevailing more in this world; you may feel that you could do more yourself; but also that circumstances may make this somewhat awkward. You could, though, make more efforts in that direction, with some confidence that you could make things work well.

The higher values of life, which are the spiritual values by which the soul aspires to live in this life, have their own positive creative intelligence and organizing power, and all of this is at your disposal if you would but choose to use it. To do this requires that you identify yourself more as the soul that you are; in doing so, you will quite spontaneously find the right opportunities at the right time for you to be the right person, in the right place, to do the right thing, without it having any undesirable consequences. You just need to have a more conscious confidence in yourself as a soul, able to draw upon the resources you seek.

Score 11 - 20

This is a very good score when balanced with a strong ego which is firmly under your control. If so, you are giving yourself to others without losing control of your life.

You probably feel that, overall, you've got things working well. You seem to have things under control, whilst at the same time able to be generous towards a wide range of contenders for your attention. You have the energy and mental and spiritual resources to cope with whatever comes along.

You know that you're a loving person, and you deeply cherish being able to love those in your life and others for whom you're able to give love in a way that's appropriate for their needs at the time.

It may be your desire to love more, which it probably is, then you would seek to know how you could do this. You could do this by placing your ego more within your soul, and use the organizing power of your soul to bring about the resources, synchronicities, circumstances and opportunities which will allow you to love more without taking away from anyone or anything else.

Your spiritual journey requires as much forethought and organization as any journey you would take in the physical world. Your journeys through the physical world, to judge by your score in this exercise, are going well. What kind of spiritual journeys are you taking?

Score: 21 and over:

It's inevitable when you're such a giving and spiritually-oriented person that people's expectations of you may become excessive, draining you of energy, time, money and any other resources which you can put their way. You may end up short of everything including your patience and love for them. It's crucially important, therefore, that you have a strong enough ego to be able to achieve and maintain a workable balance.

That's especially the case where your generosity is really more a response to a sense of duty or obligation to support other people, rather than your love, even unconditional love, for them.

However, being the spiritually-centered person that you are, you should be finding that resources come your way as needed, and you can be quite re-laxed about giving to others from your inexhaustible wealth of abundance.

You may already have come to the conclusion that "enough is enough" and you have enough, and somehow the universe contrives always to supply enough. It's more a case of managing your "enough-ness" so that you have enough, can give enough and can receive enough to be able to maintain that same workable balance which the universe maintains in its apparently ef-fortless and infinite, unconditionally loving, dispensation of abundant life.

Lecture 4: Section Conclusion

It is my belief, based on my understandings and experience, that the more we are oriented towards ourselves as a soul, accessing the greater, spiritual dimensions of our life, the more we will draw upon love, and the more love we will express, give to others, and feel within ourselves. Also, in drawing upon the greater, spiritual dimensions of life, we will draw upon the most positive, uplifting, constructive and holistic organizing power of life, which will be for everyone's benefit, not just our own. Hence the purpose of this course, to inspire, encourage and enable you to do that - to love more, and specifically to draw on the greater spiritual dimensions of your life for the benefits it brings to you and others.

I'd now like to go on in the next section to discuss the practical ways in which you could love more.

---

7. ARE YOU A "SERVICE TO SELF" OR "SERVICE TO OTHERS" PERSON?

Lecture 1: Section Introduction

Mahatma Gandhi said: "The best way to find yourself is to lose yourself in the service of others".

It is said that there are only two types of people in the world; one can be called "Service to Self" and the other can be called "Service to Others". Also it is said that if more than half the people in the world were "Service to Others", the world would be a very different place indeed.

A "Service to Self" person is one who is primarily concerned in his or her everyday life with himself or herself. Such a person could reasonably be called selfish, self-centered, preoccupied with their own affairs. You would not take it for granted that such a person would be very helpful, whenever asked, unless there was money for them to make, and they're probably better left well alone. Or you could give it a try, but don't be too surprised if you get turned down.

It's more than likely that such a person would be more oriented towards their ego than their soul. Such a person would not readily extend their love to others, except for their own advantage; when, of course, it wouldn't really be love.

A "Service to Others" person, on the other hand, is primarily concerned with the interests of others, which could mean other people, whether individuals, communities, nations; with animals, nature in all its forms, the environment, the planet and so on. This is the sort of person who you might imagine would be helpful, whenever asked. And potentially somewhat over-burdened by too many people's expectations, which they ought to avoid becoming!

It's more than likely that such a "Service to Others" person would be more oriented towards their soul than their ego.   Such a person would readily extend their love to others, and it would be real love.

Therefore, one may say that "Service to Others" is a higher kind of love than "Service to Self". We can look that a little closer because it may not be so straightforward.

We can look a little closer by considering how one might become less of a "Service to Self" person and more of a "Service to Others" person.

In this way we can learn some of the ways in which we can love more, specifically in ways which would be beneficial and pleasurable for others, whilst also making it a beneficial and pleasurable experience for oneself. Love relationships don't work well if they are too one-sided.

However, this is not quite as straightforward as one might imagine. And there are some pitfalls to be avoided when you're giving your love, in some circumstances, and this section, this "Service to Self" versus "Service to Others" section, is a good place to address these things. Let's go on to the next lecture.

Lecture 2: Becoming less "Service to Self"

The thing about loving other people, especially in relation to how it impacts upon other people, is that it isn't necessarily welcomed by them, and it isn't necessarily the best thing for them.

We need to be aware of what we're doing when we're loving other people.

For instance, the other person might not want your love, or might feel indebted to you in some way, that either they can't repay for some reason, or simply don't want to, and therefore might feel uncomfortable about being on the receiving end of your love, in whatever form it takes.

Also there are times when it's not appropriate to help people; it may be better that they learn to take responsibility for themselves, or in some other way do something, or learn to be something on their own, without anybody's help. Sometimes it's difficult to know what the situation is that one is feeling like becoming involved in, giving one's help to, giving one's love to.

Sometimes the more loving thing is to stand back, or walk away, and watch the train wreck, figuratively speaking, from a good distance; whilst, if it's appropriate, being prepared to come in later and offer the kind of love that might be more appropriate and welcome at that stage.

Sometimes it's easier not to extend your love to people; sometimes it's easier to avoid getting involved with other people; sometimes it's the right thing not to get involved.

So you might say, with some justification, that it's better to be a Service to Self type of person, because when you're looking after yourself, you're not depending on other people's help so much, you're taking responsibility for yourself, and you're keeping out of other peoples way. Certainly, there's something to be said for that.

However when you're spending your life in that way, you're separating yourself from the rest of the world; and that is not consistent with being a spiritual soul, connected through spirit, with everyone and everything. It's probably not going to be consistent with your soul's purpose; you're living a life which is not what your soul intended for you in this life; what you're doing is living the life of your ego. That is, unless you're striking a *proper balance* between taking responsibility for yourself and taking responsibility for others.

The proper balance is that you *do* take responsibility for yourself, and you *do* take responsibility for others, as is appropriate in your circumstances.

For instance, in the developed world, we may be living as part of a family; the family would expect us, once we are out of the total dependency of early childhood, to be taking some responsibility for ourselves - keeping our bedroom tidy; behaving well at school, learning our lessons, developing social skills at home and with friends. Whilst this is going on, our parents are looking after our well being, earning money to keep us housed and fed and clothed - taking responsibility for us.

As we get older, our parents increasingly expect us to take more responsibility for ourselves, eventually becoming independent, at which point our responsibility for ourselves becomes more or less total. And at which point you might feel it's best to be more "Service to Self" oriented, because you need to create a solid basis for your life.

In less developed parts of the world, it may be that we live in a tribe, in which case, the tribe will look after us as we grow up, but we may have to start becoming responsible within the tribe quite early; and as we get older we may need to continue to take responsibility within the tribe whilst, at the same time, the tribe is taking responsibility for us; it's a give and take situation for the whole tribe; the tribe needs everyone to play their part. At which point you might feel that it's best to be more "Service to Others" oriented, because it will work better for the tribe and for yourself.

And you might say that even in the developed world, the same is true - the community needs us to play our part; though the way this works is that we pay taxes so that the Government, local or national, provides a lot of the infrastructure and basic services for us. Equally, if we're a member of a group of some sort, or working for a company, it might serve our purposes best if we were "Service to Others" oriented.

So, even though we may appear to be "Service to Self" oriented, we might expect to have to contribute to the "other" in order for our life to work smoothly. Then we *are* creating something of a balance between taking responsibility for ourselves and for others, even though we may think we're taking out more than we're putting in. Actually we're all taking out more than we're putting in; that's the way life works; that's the benefit of being part of a greater whole.

What, therefore, would be the benefit to us in becoming less "Service to Self" oriented?

The benefit would be enormous because we would be living more as a soul, drawing on the greater, spiritual whole for its resources and organizing power, to create something far better than we have now, if we're living more as an ego which is mostly detached from the spiritual whole, and not living the purpose of our soul.

So let's see what it means to be more "Service to Others" oriented, in the next lecture.

Lecture 3: Becoming More "Service To Others" Oriented

You may already be more "Service to Others" oriented.

If you have taken responsibilities in your family, such as bringing up children, or looking after elderly parents, you may already be STO oriented, and a considerable part of your life is devoted to those responsibilities.

You may have a responsible position at work, with lots of employees and customers, and owners or shareholders, you may be a teacher or work in some organization where you have big responsibilities of one sort or another. You probably feel that your life is devoted to other people's needs, and if you like things being that way, you're probably STO oriented.

There are one of two things I'd like to discuss with you, in the interests of helping you to be more loving in your STO role, and helping you to access the resources and organizing power of the greater spiritual whole, which should make your life easier, more fulfilling and more rewarding.

Let's take these things one at a time:

How open is your heart? Does your STO role stir your heart, give you that warm glow in your heart that fills your day with pleasure?

Do you truly feel that your STO is a labour of love in which your love is the driving force behind all your STO activities?

Do you find that your STO activities work smoothly, effortlessly and are supported well by others and even, seemingly, by the universe or life itself because sometimes things happen in the most wonderful, timely, coincidental and synchronous way?

Or, on the contrary, you find that your STO activities tire you out. You feel you're taken advantage of, abused, even, and actually you don't enjoy what you're doing. Things don't work out all that well.

Do you, in fact, do your STO out of duty, obligations, pressure from others, force of circumstances, being driven by your ego to earn a higher status, or more wealth, or other factors which mean that there really isn't much love there, is there?

So, what we're looking for here is to change your STO into something much more positive, a greater expression of love, more spiritually uplifting for yourself and others, more life-supporting, drawing more on the beneficence of the universe, and more in keeping with what your soul desires for you.

Your present circumstances may really be no barrier to any of this. It may be that all you need to do is to agree that you want your life to be more fulfilling and enjoyable in those ways, and then set about considering how you can do this in your present circumstances.

For example you can use some of the methods I've suggested to help you learn to love more. You may find lots of opportunities in your present circumstances to love more. In fact, this is probably the key to changing the whole complexion of your STO.

Your circumstances may respond extremely well to the greater love that you're expressing.

On the other hand, you may find that you get abused more, with people laying even more expectations on you, which you would rightly feel are just not right. It may be that your circumstances, all the circumstances in which you are working, just don't lend themselves to responding appropriately to your loving STO. In which case, there may be no alternative to either saying, "no", or getting yourself out of those circumstances. It's not easy to say "no", especially for someone who likes doing things for others, but it's important that you say "no" when it's appropriate.

So it's up to you to judge whether your STO is genuinely an expression of your love and your soul's desire, or it's you doing things out of necessity, duty, obligation, pressure from others, pressure from your ego or some other circumstance which really isn't stirring your heart in the right way, which you really don't enjoy, and isn't really love.

When you look at your situation in that way, you'd find it productive to work out how you can improve things for yourself, whilst also finding ways of being STO, giving other people the benefit of your heartfelt love, and helping the world out in some way.

Lecture 4: Section Conclusion

What the world needs now, is love, heartfelt love. There are difficult situations and circumstances all over the place which need to be transformed by the uplifting power of love. You may know that, and you may want to do something about it. If so, you need to go about it in the right way. You know what that means; it means looking for a Win-Win situation where there are benefits on both sides.

"Service to Others" is clearly an expression of love; it goes beyond serving your own interests, even if you could justify that kind of serving in terms of taking responsibility for yourself. It's good to take responsibility for yourself. It's even better if you can take some responsibility for others as well. You could look at it as a higher kind of love, the kind we need to aspire to as we develop ourselves as part of that human society and part of the greater spiritual whole.

Remember, though, that balance between "Service to Others" and "Service to Self" is important. Strive to achieve an appropriate balance for the circumstances you're in.

Now, or later when you're ready, we'll go on to the next section where we can look at various ways in which you can express and enjoy your loving more.

8. THE PRACTICAL APPLICATIONS OF LOVE

Lecture 1: Section Introduction

In this section we're going to look at how you can love more in your life; whether at home with your family and with your friends; at work or in a group of some sort of which you're a member; in your world at large, that is, the larger world in which you live and participate; this could mean your sphere of interest and your sphere of influence even encompassing the entire world, say, for example, the world environment as a whole, or injustices around the world that you would like to help address.

But before we consider how you might sort the world out, let's start by looking at how much you love, and do justice to, yourself.

Lecture 2: Love For Yourself

Earlier on in the course we looked at how you can understand who you really are. We discovered that what the religions have been telling us, that there is a spiritual dimension to our lives, can also be understood in more scientific terms, as our consciousness being located in the field of life which is pure, self-sustaining energy and creative intelligence, that is, in the transcendental field or the unified field of natural law.

We have an individualized consciousness which, for want of a more scientific word, we can understand to be a soul. We are a soul. We gain a body, and a mind, as we are born into this world. Mind, body and soul, or spirit, in one amazing package, if you like.

What does this say about who we are? Unless we are going to deny that there is that spiritual dimension to our lives, in which our soul or spirit is located; unless we are saying that our consciousness is merely the outcome of our brain's activity, as many scientists believe, then we must recognize that our soul is part of a larger consciousness, or spirit; that our non-physical soul has an interface with that larger, spiritual dimension, and has access to all of it. And therefore you might reasonably say that this confirms what the religions have said, that we are children of the creator, so to speak. Actually, literally, but in a form we find difficult to imagine.

So, when we look in the mirror, do we see ourselves as a body or a soul? If we see ourselves as a body, we probably have some complaints about how we look. If we see ourselves as a soul, we recognize ourselves to be awesome beyond our own understanding, and worthy of the most intense love we can conjure up in our hearts. Wouldn't this be a good way to start the day?

If we can see ourselves first and foremost as a spiritual soul, and awesome beyond our ability to imagine, we ought to love ourselves with a love which is unconditional and without bounds. We should have a lot more respect for ourselves. We should recognize that we have no idea of our own potential, especially now that we recognize that we can draw on the energy and creative intelligence of the spiritual dimension of our life. We should take more responsibility for ourselves and what we do. We should recognize that we have a purpose in our lives which is worthwhile, not just for ourselves but for others too, and we should know what our purpose is, rather than exercising our free will to do whatever our ego wants us to do.

Looking at ourselves like this as we look into the mirror in the morning should give us a pretty good start to the day. Your eyes are the window to your soul. So when you look into the mirror, look into your eyes and say, "I love me."

Lecture 3: Love With Family And Friends

In the last lecture I asked you to look at yourself with unconditional love, as the awesome soul that you really are. Could you look at your family and friends in the same way?

It's very easy to get caught up in personalities, and all the dynamics of family life. But if we were to see each other as spiritual souls, all equal in status as part of that greater spiritual consciousness of which we're all part, all growing as souls through life's experiences, all with a worthwhile and important purpose in our lives, even though we may not know what each other's purpose is, we should be able to relate to each other more on the level of their soul than their personality or ego. And in that way, the basis of our relationships with each other should be one of unconditional love.

We do, of course, also relate to each other on the basis of conditional love, that is we enjoy each other in a great variety of ways, not least in the case of families, on the basis that we are members of the same family, and that sense of belonging to the family is important to us. "I love you because you are my mother, my father, brother, sister, son, daughter, whatever." This is a valid and powerful reason to love, and should not be under-valued by comparison with the unconditional soul love that you have added as the basis to the more conditional forms of love.

Family relations offer opportunities for the most intense expressions and experiences of love. One's spouse or partner, one would hope would be the focus of the most intense love, physically and emotionally; children also can be loved almost more than one can bear; mother, father, brother, sister can be loved, even through all the years of dysfunction that many families suffer.

Even so, the knowledge that we are all spiritual souls should add more of the unconditionality of love within the family. Whenever you find your love is overshadowed by day-to-day events, even by the rigors of family life over the years, your unconditional love should shine like a sun that never sets.

The same should apply with friends, who are close enough to your heart to enjoy an ongoing, loving relationship with; your recognition of them as souls, and your unconditional love for them as souls, should make the light of your conditional love shine ever more brightly.

Lecture 4: Love At Work Or In Groups

As I said in the last lecture, your appreciation of people as spiritual souls like yourself should enable you to shine the light of unconditional love in any relationships, and now I'd like to include the connections or interactions you have at work or in a group where you're a member.

Here I'm most interested in showing you the benefits of loving more within a group, whether at work or otherwise where there is a group activity or objective going on.

You know the idea that a group can be greater than the sum of its parts, at least potentially. You know there is such a thing as "team spirit" which helps the team to achieve more, and football coaches for example are always working to increase team spirit and cohesion.

It's true that groups can achieve more than individuals. Certainly it's true that individuals can achieve some really amazing things on their own, such as writing a bestselling book or creating a wonderful work of art.

But a group can draw on a great deal of creative organizing power which somehow makes things work more effectively, faster and more effortlessly. This can happen when there is a specific purpose to which all the group are committed and have the skills to achieve or can draw on the resources they need. This can only happen, though, when group is very cohesive and focused. It won't happen when members of the group are at each other's throats, arguing, competing with each other and generally making the group work difficult.

The quality of group interaction that will give rise to the level of cohesiveness or team spirit that is needed to generate this X factor for success is love. Love in the sense of fellowship and sharing of the group objectives, openness and honesty in one's interactions with group members, respect, appreciation, tolerance, generosity, helpfulness, gratitude, understanding, sincerity, courtesy, persistence and a deep sense of togetherness and other qualities which can bind the group together.

This group cohesion generates an organizing power which draws on the creative intelligence of life itself. Synchronicity develops from which surprisingly beneficial things can happen. Amazing coincidences can happen. A sense that the group activity has a momentum of its own which makes everything happen very easily becomes pervasive, ever-present. There's a sense that the feeling that goes with this does not happen when one is on one's own or working with a group which is not cohesive and focused in that way.

So I recommend that when you are working with other people you can contribute significantly to the success of the groups work by offering as much love as you can to the group, your unconditional love in recognition that you are all awesome spiritual souls, and by offering the various qualities that I mentioned earlier such as respect, appreciation, tolerance and so on.

I'm sure, having experienced that sort of thing myself, you would find it very enjoyable and satisfying. In fact you may always want to be with a group working in that way, rather than being on your own.

This goes to show that if whole communities, nations, the world even, were to share a wonderful objective, and work at it together, they could move mountains together, very easily.

I'll talk some more about this in the next lecture.

Lecture 5: Love In Your World

Lots of us want to change the world. Some of us want to change a little bit of it, such as our local community, some of us want to change the whole world.

If you want to change some of the world, realistically-speaking you need a group. It could be your group that you would start, or someone else's group that you would join, or a group that you would support in some way.

I spoke in the last lecture about how you can help to make a group stronger, and what the attributes of a strong group are. I said that the qualities of love are the ones which best help groups to achieve the cohesiveness and team spirit to help them achieve their objectives.

A woman by the name of Margaret Mead who was a well-known commentator in America in the 1960s and 70s is said to have said, "Never doubt that a small group of thoughtful, committed citizens can change the world. Indeed, it is the only thing that ever has."

I agree with that, that it's possible for a small group to achieve very big things. But they could only do that, I believe, if they were highly cohesive, skilled and focused on their objectives.

Better still, a larger group, but the larger the group the more difficult it is to achieve the necessary degree of cohesion. Perhaps it's better that a number of smaller, highly cohesive groups who share the same objective would work together, harmonizing their various skills.

Back in the early 1990s, I was a member, one of the first members, of a group whose mission was to learn, and teach, how to create unity within groups and between groups. This was primarily to create healing groups, but the principles would apply to other groups too.

This was after I had been a member of the consciousness-raising groups practicing Yogic Flying, as I described earlier. And after I'd had some even earlier experiences of the power of cohesive groups. I've added a file to the Resources section of this lecture in which I've described my various experiences with groups; it's worth reading because my experiences have been quite extraordinary, and they are part of the key to why I feel qualified to write this course with its emphasis on living as a soul and drawing from the greater, spiritual dimension of life.

So I'm aware of the value of being a member of a cohesive group, and aware of how such cohesion can be achieved. For our purposes here, I would distill the various methods of achieving cohesion, or unity, within a group into one method: love.

If you want to change the world, or some part of the world, and you know the particular thing you want to change, and you know how it can be done, find a group to do it with, a group which has the same objective as yourself; support it with your love, whether that means working directly with it, or using their platform if it helps you and them achieve complementary objectives, as I'm doing here, or supporting it in some way, financially, or giving them your time and skills, or signing up to their campaigns, and so on. However you do it, do it first and foremost in the spirit of love.

Resources:

Love As Organizing Power

In this lecture, I said I'd say something about the experiences I've had that made me realize the power of living and working in a more unified state of being and doing, the basis of which is love, in one expression or another, e.g. service, unity.

This is what has enabled me to identify love as a tremendously powerful organizing principle that can make amazingly good things happen.

The primary key to these experiences has been the unity, or unified state of being, that I was in. That might not sound like love, and my experiences, as I describe them, won't sound like love. But in this course, I'm asking you to love from a unified state of being; that is, from the level of your soul which is, in itself, in a unified state of being with all there is, and is an embodiment, or an ensoulment, of love.

Your soul, being located in the spiritual dimension of your life, in what I'm also calling the transcendental field of consciousness, is part of the whole of life and totally unified with it. When I'm asking you to identify yourself as a soul, and to live as a soul, I'm saying that this will naturally align you with that more unified state of being.

So here are some experiences I've had of that more unified state of being.

My earliest experience, that I was conscious of, was at the age of 12, back in 1957, when I recognized that people in society weren't caring enough about other people; didn't love each other enough. That was my unified state of mind, in a state of unity or empathy with those who weren't being loved enough. I discovered much later, 40-odd years later, that when you're thinking in a unified state of mind, the memory stays with you much longer; and I do still clearly remember the thought I had at that time:

"I'm going to spend the rest of my life sorting that out", which I'm still doing, more than 60 years later.

The desire to help other people, to serve them, to give them a good experience, has stayed with me through my life and there have been many instances of good things happening for me; I've often felt that I've lived a blessed life, though I can't say for certain that it's because I've maintained some degree of that unity with other people that comes from wanting to serve people well. That's being a "Service To Others" kind of person, as I've described in this course. I think it does make good things happen.

Some experiences I can relate that do show definite results are as follows:

In the early 1970s I was co-owner of a small hotel in Edinburgh. Things weren't going well because we had two periods when the British economy was going through crises with the coal miners striking for higher wages, and everyone had their power supplies reduced to just three days a week. It had a crippling effect on our restaurant trade, at a time when we were struggling anyway, having spent all our capital and not having enough in reserve to weather any downturn of that sort.

Clearly, I thought, rightly or wrongly, there's something wrong with the way the economy works that it should come to this sort of crisis point. We were faced with making decisions: should we lower our prices, perhaps change our style to something more like fast food than the expensive food we were offering? It made me ask a question that changed my whole approach.

"Surely," I asked myself, "there must be a way of making spontaneous right decisions? By being aligned somehow to some universal intelligence whereby every decision is right; where I can be the right person in the right place at the right time doing the right thing in the right way?"

Shortly after that, I was running the catering for a big event taking place in Edinburgh. It was an International Congress which involved numerous major international companies who were exhibiting their products there. We were commissioned to provide catering for three of these companies on quite a large scale over the course of four days. This included a no-expense-spared wine and food buffet for over 1000 people at the most prestige venue in Edinburgh.

During the course of the four days, when I was driving back and forth across Edinburgh to the various venues where we were catering, I got the feeling that everything was going extremely well. It was almost as if the traffic lights were turning green for me as I drove through the city streets. All the catering went perfectly; this was on a far bigger scale than I had handled before, and yet everything was going incredibly well. I felt different; I felt very calm and good inside. At the end of the event I said to my partner, "I don't know what happened this week, but this is how I want it to be all the time, and I'm not going to do anything else until I've discovered what it was that made it happen like that."

I realized much later that what had happened was that I had experienced the benefits of working together with people who were very focused on making a big success of the week, and were generating a powerful, unified state of working together, with which I was working and therefore a part of it. The good feeling I'd had during the week was something that I became accustomed to a few years later.

Those questions I asked myself stayed with me for the next two or three years until one day I thought, "I need to find out what my potential is," and after that, "I need to be who I really am."

A very short time after that, I met someone who was practicing transcendental meditation. I asked him what it was about, and he said, "It's about fulfilling your potential." Actually he could have said, "It's about relieving stress," which is how most people were selling it at the time, but he said exactly what I wanted to hear. I took a course of instruction in transcendental meditation that very same week.

At that time, a new, more advanced form of transcendental meditation, and now popularly known as yogic flying, was being taught. It was said to raise the collective consciousness of a country when a very small number of people were practicing yogic flying as a group. I decided I would like to become a yogic flyer to find out whether this would help me to find the answer to my questions.

Indeed, it did. It also gave me an experience that very few people have had, when I experienced what it was like to work when a large group of yogic flyers were raising consciousness together.

A community for yogic flyers had been set up in Skelmersdale, a town in the North West of England, and I moved there when the community first started. By virtue of my experience in catering, I was asked to manage the catering for the large events we held there, usually over weekends when up to 800 people would be "flying" together.

My experience over numerous of these events over the next 10 years was always the same. On the day when people were traveling to the event, say, on the Friday, everything would become very awkward. We used to say, "it's like working in mud." Everything would feel disorganized, chaotic, and everyone would be feeling tense. It seems that we were feeling the effects of all the people who were traveling to the weekend event, in their unsettled states of mind.

On the Saturday, as the "flyers" were settling down, things on the catering side were coming together better, and the catering staff were settling down too.

And then by late Saturday, and on the Sunday, when the flyers were extremely deep in meditation, I got the same feeling that I'd had those years before when I was driving across Edinburgh and the traffic lights were turning green for me. I felt very calm and good. It was the same feeling, and this same feeling happened reliably every single time that I was running the catering for these big yogic flying events.

So it's very clear in my mind that when we achieve a more unified state of being, we find that things will happen in a very good way. They will be beneficial for a lot of people. The organizing power that the unified state of being generates is inclusive, in that good things happen for everyone who is affected by that unified state of being.

Later, after I left the yogic flying community at the end of the 1980s, I joined a couple of friends to start a clinical practice aiming to create unity within groups. My friends had also been yogic flyers but, like myself, were no longer practicing yogic flying. During the time I was with them, and afterwards as I continued to be a member of the group, I continued to have experiences of the benefits of that unified state.

And since then, whilst I've been largely on my own, I haven't experienced those same, very pronounced feelings and benefits that come from being with a powerfully unified group. I have however, continued in a service role, firstly looking after my widowed mother for 12 years to 2004, and being chairman of an older people's campaigning organization to 2009; and since then working to understand the massive shift of consciousness which has been widely expected to happen at this time. And I should say that during these years away from the yogic flying group, I have still felt very blessed and have had some amazing things happening in my life, for which I give credit to my desire to live from as deep a part of myself as I can, namely as a spiritual soul, with my heart open, aiming to be of service to others and generally being as loving as I can.

The whole direction of my life since leaving the yogic flying group has been to help people everywhere to rise to a higher level of consciousness, without them having to be yogic flyers or meditators themselves. And for them to navigate these present years of rising consciousness in the most comfortable way; which I have deduced to be to learn to love more, hence the name of this course.

Perhaps not surprisingly, this takes me back to that time nearly 60 years ago when I recognized that people don't love each enough and thought, in words that I clearly remember thinking, "I'm going to spend the rest of my life sorting that out!"

Lecture 6: The Law Of Attraction

On a slightly different tack, there's another way in which you can use your love beneficially.

You've probably heard people talking about "The Law Of Attraction".

They're talking about something that has become popular in recent years, though it's something that has always been talked about and applied in one way or another, such as through prayer, or making a wish but it's now also called "The Law Of Attraction". Fortunately neither prayer nor making wishes nor the law of attraction work instantly. It's just as well. Imagine what the world would be like if our wishes came true instantly. Even so, the law of attraction ought to come with some words of caution, such as: "Be careful what you wish for, for it will surely be yours."

The modern version of "The Law Of Attraction" offers a variety of techniques to help you attract what you want in your life.

My own feeling is that indeed we should be careful what we wish for, for it will surely be ours.

I want to offer a suggestion which you will see fits happily into the context of this course, because it urges you to use your love at the level of your soul in order to attract what you want.

It seems to me that most people who use the law of attraction do so from the level of their ego. As Janis Joplin sang, "Oh Lord, won't you buy me a Mercedes-Benz, my friends all have Porsches, I must make amends". The law of attraction certainly does work if you persist with your determination to attract something into your life, if you visualize it as if you already have it, if you take whatever action could contribute towards attracting it (such as earning enough money to buy it) but how often will it be that you find that it doesn't bring you the joy you expected, and will turn out to be burden for you or not appropriate for you in some way. This is what can happen when you allow your ego to use The Law Of Attraction.

A much safer way to attract things, and a much surer way of attracting the right things in your life, is to attract from level of your soul.

If you pay attention to what your soul is encouraging you to do, you will more likely find that you are guided to attract into your life exactly what you need, no more, no less, in the fastest conceivable time, with the least effort and with the least expenditure. You will not regret attracting such things into your life. You may never get your Mercedes-Benz but you could be thankful that you didn't. It might only have brought you grief in the end.

The law of attraction is therefore a very good exercise for you. You should always be paying attention to what your soul is guiding you to do. Your soul is always guiding you in the spirit of love, and in the same spirit of love, your ego, that part of you which lives outwardly in this material world, should allow that soul part of you to guide your ego's actions in the outer world and also to manage the hidden machinations of life that will cooperate together to help bring what your heart and soul desire in the most wonderfully effortless way you could imagine.

In the Resources section of this lecture you'll find an exercise to do, with guidelines to follow. But I'll run through the guidelines now so that I can cover the main points with you.

Firstly, as I said earlier, we need to recognize that the part of us that is our soul, is very heavily invested in this life, and can be trusted to help us attract into our life what is best for us. The soul always acts in a spirit of love, and will never attract something that is less than the best for us. So we should be open to what our soul would bring into our life, if we would but pay attention to what it is offering.

We should at all times be attentive to what the soul has in mind for this life of ours. We have free will certainly, and our soul will not interfere with our ego and its self-created motivations; but our soul is the one we should be listening to. So before trying to bring anything else into your life, spend some time working out what your life is all about, from the point of view of your soul. This may take a little time, and should be an ongoing adventure for your ego to develop a successful partnership with your soul.

What you are looking for is the greatest expression of love in your life. This will be a good guide to what your soul is hoping for. It's probable that you will be seeking to do something which would be of great benefit to other people, to humanity, part or the whole of humanity, or to animals, some part of nature, the environment or what have you.

When you feel you have a sense of what it would be good for you to attract into your life, in those terms I've just described, that is, what your soul would most like to see in your life, create a mindset which will manifest it into your life.

That is, envisage that thing in your life in its proper context, and how it will be working. See yourself in that context, working with it in a way that makes you feel very good, fulfilled, and loving. See the results of what you are doing, in any way which shows how successful this thing is in creating the effect you're imagining.

Really put your heart into this, into the manifestation of what you are imagining. Persist with it. It may take some time, depending on what it is, and what it takes for the creative energy behind the process to manifest it in the most holistic way; that is, in such a way that the most benefit for all concerned will be created.

You'll need to take action. It's best to use the least action you'll need, because this will be most in line with the creative process you are invoking. For example, if you want some food, you should go to a food shop, reach into your pocket for the money and pay for it yourself. If you already have the money, or any other thing, you don't need to magically manifest it from somewhere else. That's even if you think you're running short of money to buy something else tomorrow. You need to develop confidence in the process you are learning how to use. You may find that the thing that you thought you would need money for tomorrow, you no longer need the money for because someone has given it to you, or you didn't need it after all.

You need to be aware of how the process of manifestation is working for you, because the confidence that you develop is part of the manifestation process.

So use the law of attraction. Use it because it is part of the creative process of life, and you yourself are nothing if not creative. Know that you can create. Remember that the creative force is love. Create with love, if you would create the very best thing for you.

Resources:

Law Of Attraction Exercise:

Here is an exercise for you to practice the Law of Attraction.

As a first exercise, you should aim to attract something fairly easy to attract, and then progressively work up to attract things that you would normally think difficult to attract.

As I emphasized in the lecture, it's much better that you attract something at the level of your soul, not from your ego (like the proverbial Mercedes Benz) so, what would your soul think of attracting?

You can decide for yourself, but could I suggest that, for example, you might aim to attract opportunities to be kind to others? That would be a worthwhile thing to attract.

Perhaps you might aim to attract such opportunities in circumstances where you wouldn't normally go looking for such opportunities, such as in public places.

So, remember the methodology:

1. Aim to attract something from the level of your soul e.g., as just described above

2. Make this something that is congruent with what you believe your soul purpose could be, e.g., bringing more kindness into the world; or the greatest expression of love you could hope to exhibit

3. Generate some real enthusiasm for being kind to someone

4. Envisage yourself in the circumstances you have chosen to attract something into, e.g. yourself in a public place, with lots of people around.

5. Envisage yourself in the mindset that you'd be in if you were going to be kind to someone

6. Take action, by putting yourself into that situation, e.g., go into the city center.

7. Without limiting yourself by envisaging a *detailed* scenario and circumstances that could produce the opportunity you're looking for, imagine putting yourself forward to be kind to someone, in some way (it could be as simple as smiling or saying 'hi!'' to someone whom you can see would appreciate a kind gesture)

8. Envisage the good feeling it would give you when you've done an act of kindness; and envisage the other person feeling good about it too.

9. Be ready to really put your heart into your act of kindness; and when the opportunity arises, put your heart into it.

10. When the opportunity arises, go for it because you know you attracted it into your life; make the most of the opportunity

11. When it's done, thank your higher self for having created that situation where the opportunity has arisen (it may seem as if you mostly created it yourself, but your higher self or soul may have steered you in the right direction for you to see an opportunity).

12. Recognize that you made the Law of Attraction work for you and, when you're ready, aim to do it again.

13. Don't push yourself too fast, because the confidence you get from attracting small things into your life will create a strong foundation for bigger things. You need to create that strong foundation; if you're too ambitious too early, you'll fail to develop the confidence which is part of your ability to create, or attract.

Lecture 7 Section Conclusion

In this section we've looked at how you can love in various spheres of your life, spheres ranging from loving yourself, through family and friends, people at work and in groups, all the way up to putting your love to work in the entire world to change things on a global scale.

You'll have noticed the words "unconditional love" and "soul" coming up time and again, and that's because loving the unconditional love from the level of your soul is the key to living the good life, and loving the good life.

Unconditional love is the quality of love that your soul loves; unconditional love is the soul's nature, and spirit, as it is life's nature and spirit too.

When we love unconditionally from the level of the soul, we have a sound basis for all our activities and all our relationships. Let any kind of aspect, or quality, of love, and any kind of conditional, "because" kind of love sit on the top of your unconditional love, and if there is no incongruence, no inconsistency, there, then you have a right basis for how you're doing your loving.

Unconditional love means love without condition, and this can be given only by the soul which is the very embodiment of unconditional love, the soul which is part of life itself, an individualized spark of that life whose nature and spirit is love - love which is sufficient unto itself, infinite, universal and unconditional.

Without that foundation of unconditional love, expressed as the spirit of your soul, you would have an uncertain basis for your loving.

———————————————

9. YOUR WORLD OF LOVE

Lecture 1: Section Introduction

I'm taking you on a journey to greater and greater expressions of love. What I mean by that is a greater and greater framework in which you can express your love. At every stage of this journey, you'll be doing the same thing, only more so; you simply need to love; love more than before, and love more in more contexts than before.

The greater framework I'm explaining to you will give you a sense of the greater framework of your life in which you live, for example the spiritual dimensions of your life, and the groups, communities, nations and the whole Earth in which you live and interact in whatever ways you do; and also a sense of the power that your love can have when expressed in those different areas of your life.

I'm going to take a giant leap for mankind now by looking at the largest framework that I know of, which I feel is appropriate to discuss with you in this course, and also the greatest power that I believe you realistically can draw upon with your love.

To do this I'm going to draw on what I've learnt through my studies, what my observations have been regarding the validity of what I've learnt, and my experiences of how this knowledge can work in everyday life.

Most of this largest framework has to be a matter for conjecture and speculation, in rather the same way that the religions teach their teachings, asking for your faith and belief, and the scientists develop their theories about things that are *way* beyond our ability to see for ourselves, and they do their best to prove them to us; but by being open to these teachings and theories, and observing how they are regarded by the experts in the field, also by learning about people's experiences of such things, one can *infer* the truth or otherwise. And inference is a valid way of gaining knowledge.

I was told many years ago, by someone I respect, that I should never be dogmatic. I've learnt that that was very good advice. If I really don't know for sure what I'm talking about, or even if I am sure in some cases, I shouldn't express myself as if what I'm talking about is absolute, incontestable, incontrovertible fact.

With that caveat in mind, let me take you where no man has gone before; well, at least, where not very many men and women have gone before.

I'm going to put it to you that you are life itself, living itself. You have the DNA of life, that is, the spiritual DNA of life, so to speak, within you.

You are not the whole of life, but part of life. Some scientists say that life is holographic, that is, when you break the hologram into pieces, each piece mirrors the whole of the hologram. Other scientists say that life is fractal, which means that each new piece is a perfect replica, though smaller, of the whole.

To justify this, I am going to discuss again, who you really are, by drawing on a number of different life views, or conceptions of what life is, in the next lecture. And then, I'm going to discuss the implications of this for you, in your life, and demonstrate to you what I said at the very beginning of the course that, truly, you are an embodiment of love.

Lecture 2: Who Are You Really? - Pt 2

Earlier in the course, I asked you to consider who you are, really. I asked you to see beyond your outer personality, your ego, and all the labels we all apply to ourselves, our name, our occupation, our faith, gender, sexuality and so on; and to recognize that first and foremost we are a spiritual being, an individual soul or spirit, with a consciousness which is part of a greater spiritual consciousness; and we have a body in which we live our life in this physical, material world. Who we are really, we discussed, is a spiritual soul, an individualized piece, or part, of spirit.

www.andrewnewberg.com/research

Can Science Explain the Soul?
https://www.huffingtonpost.com/deepak-chopra/can-science-ex-plain-the-s_b_675107.html
https://www.sfgate.com/opinion/chopra/article/Can-science-ex-plain-the-soul-2463078.php

But is that all we can say about ourselves? If we are an individualized spirit, how do we relate to the greater whole of spirit? How did we become an individualized spirit, a soul?

And what does this mean? Is there some purpose to us becoming an individualized spirit, or were we something that somehow just fell off or fell out of the greater wholeness of spirit? And if so, does our life really count for anything, or can we live it as if the world is our oyster, to do with what we will, so to speak?

Let's look at some of the teachings from various sources which can offer us a sense of who we really are, where do we come from, how long have we got?

I should say before I start that this lecture may get pretty heavy, going quite deeply into religion and science. I'll be summarizing what it has taken me decades to understand. If you decide to give this lecture a miss, I won't blame you one bit. It will be enough if you can take it from me that you truly are an embodiment of love, as I started this course by saying. And as an embodiment of love, you can help make the world go round a lot more smoothly than it does. If you really take that to heart, you can skip this lecture and mark it as read.

Drawing on the Christian religion, because this is the one I'm most familiar with, there is the Christ figure, there is the Holy Trinity of which the Christ, or son, is part; the Christ is said to be the Only Be-gotten, and the Christ, in his, or its, incarnation 2000 years ago, said that for us, the kingdom of heaven is within; the Christ demonstrated unconditional, self-sacrificing love through service to mankind, compassion, forgiveness, healing, and so on, and urged us to do the same, saying that we could do the same, and more.

If Christ is the Only Begotten, and Christ was the only thing that was ever begotten, or created, and the kingdom of heaven is within us and we could do the same as he, does that mean that we are all part of the only begotten and we also must be Christ, that we have the Christ DNA within us?

The Christian church does not teach us to **be** Christ, at most it teaches us to be Christ-like, or like Jesus who it sees as the one and only Christ; at least, that's what the mainstream Christian churches teaches, to the best of my knowledge; this shows that I am not evangelizing for the Christian Church, because I don't agree with the Church in that crucial regard. However, there are some essential truths in the Christian teachings, as I have discovered for myself through other avenues than the church, and I'm going to explain those same truths from two, very different approaches to understanding life and who we are. This will help us to understand that we can connect our spiritual being with the very source of creation, in the here and now. Hence, in Christian terms, if the kingdom of heaven is within us, and we are made in the likeness of God, our love is the love of God.

Where do we see the same essential truths expressed in other ways?

Albert Einstein was one of many scientists who believed that there must be a creator of the universe, whom they may have called God, because they could see from the mathematical precision, consistency and beauty of the universe, of nature and the laws of nature that there must be an inconceivably vast, purposeful intelligence behind it.

In the Resources section of this lecture there is a link to a list of scientists who believed in God for such scientifically-considered reasons.

www.godandscience.org/apologetics/sciencefith.html

My own studies took me some years ago to a website which I mentioned earlier. It's called The Revelatorium. It publishes a work on what is called 'sacred geometry'. This describes in detail the mathematical creation of the universe. I'm not going to urge you to read this work, because it's extremely heavy reading, but if you wish to, be my guest. There's a link to it in the Resources section.

The work was compiled by a small group of people known as gnostics; gnostic means possessing spiritual knowledge which one gains through revelation, meditation, intuition and deep thinking, going so deep within that one literally accesses knowledge at its source. Generally gnostics do not belong to any mainstream religion but forge the path to the ultimate truth by themselves.

This particular work describes in detail the geometric creation of the universe. It starts with a cube which contains a sphere, representing, respectively, what they consider to be the divine feminine and divine masculine energies, that is, the Divine Mother and the Divine Father, which came together in love to create their Only Begotten Son, or Son and Daughter combined, which is the Christ. And that is the only thing, the only begotten, that the Divine Mother and Divine Father ever created.

From that point onwards, it is the internal energy and intrinsic dynamics of the Christ which gives rise to the entire manifest creations, physical and non-physical, multiple universes in multiple dimensions.

This shows that the Christ is at the heart of all living beings, physical and nonphysical. It is possible for us to fully realize, and actualize, ourselves as Christ, in what is called Christ Consciousness. This echoes what Jesus said. He himself was fully actualized as the Christ, and embodied the Christ. He was in Christ Consciousness. When he said that we can do all that he did, and more, he was saying that we too can realize, and actualize, ourselves as the Christ embodied, in our body, each of us, every one of us.

So that's another source of knowledge suggesting who we really are, from outside of the mainstream, established Christian Church and, as far as I know, any mainstream religion.

A third body of knowledge saying the same thing, that is, that we ourselves can find our source at the very point of creation of the universe, is the Vedic knowledge from ancient India.

I studied this when I was with the Transcendental Meditation group practicing yogic flying. This study was called Vedic Science. "Vedic" means from the Veda. "Veda" means understanding of the sacred.

The Veda explains how the whole of creation and the laws of nature emerge from the unmanifest, invisible, formless state of absolute pure being in a highly systematic way. It is an inconceivably sophisticated body of knowledge, said to be a revelation from the Hindu god Brahma to the sages and seers of India some 3000 years ago.

Some modern scientists have developed what Einstein in his day tried to develop but failed, namely an understanding of the ultimate, fundamental point of creation, namely a Unified Field. They have compared their formulae for creation, called the Lagrangian for the Unified Field, with the Vedic formulae for creation, despite their totally different languages, and found them to be identical.

This is another way of showing us what our source is, and who we really are at the most fundamental level of ourselves. We are part of the absolute pure being of life, expressing itself through its own creative intelligence in all that we see in the manifest creation, including ourselves.

We are therefore a *very* great deal more than we have been led to believe. And, being part of the whole scheme of creation, we have access to the creative intelligence and organizing power of life; the motive power of which is love.

So, I'm going to put it to you now, that you, in this present life of yours, in this body of yours, and in the spirit or soul which you are in the nonphysical field of life, you are an embodiment of love, that is created by love, and you have within yourself the love of the creator that you are part of. So there you have it. And so it is. Now make it so.

Resources:

1. The Revelatorium

Https://www.revelatorium.com

The Revelatorium of Alpha and Omega opens the doorway to Reality by revealing for the first time before Mankind the higher dimensional Cosmic Laws of Creation including the complete Intelligent Design by which all of Creation has been blueprinted and expressed.

The Revelatorium also reveals the basic tenets of Creation, including the natures of all eighteen dimensions under Reality.

2. Lagrangian of the Unified Field

During the past quarter century, modern physics has explored progressively more fundamental levels of nature's functioning at the atomic, nuclear and sub-nuclear scales, culminating in the recent discovery of the Unified Field - a single, universal field of nature's intelligence at the foundation of the universe.

This Unified Field, or "E8xE8 superstring field," is the crowning achievement of fifty years of advanced research in quantum gravity theory, and is expressed most concisely in a compact Lagrangian, or "super-formula," presented, for simplicity, in the super-conformal gauge.

Read more at: https://en.wikipedia.org/wiki/Lagrangian_(field_theory)

3. Vedic Formula for the Unified Field

According to Maharishi's Vedic Science the complete knowledge of the self-referral dynamics of the field of pure consciousness is available in the most ancient record of knowledge, Rk Veda and the Vedic Literature. Rk Veda and the Vedic Literature display the 'fluctuations' of the field of pure consciousness, which are spontaneously generated from the self-referral impulses (*Vrittis*) of the intelligence of the Unified Field within itself.

Read more at:

https://www.miu.edu/keepingeducationreal

Lecture 3: The Power Of Love To Make Things Happen

When you associate yourself with the creator of the universe, when you recognize that you are part of that, when you know that you have a connection to the creative intelligence and organizing power of the creator, when you know that the love of the creator runs through you, then you realize that you have access to a great deal of power to make good things happen.

When you identify yourself more and more as Spirit, as individualized Spirit, or soul, you recognize that you have a great deal of power at your disposal, and a great deal of responsibility to use it wisely, constructively, for the good of all, then you also want to know how to use the power of the love of which you, in this life, are an embodiment.

And increasingly, you want to get this right.

It's important, therefore, that you develop the relationship between the driver of your mind and body - your ego - and your soul; and between your soul and the greater spirit, the love and creative intelligence and organizing power of the universe, or the creator, if you will.

It's really important that you live increasingly as your soul, rather than as your ego. I've found that it takes quite a time to hold your ego in its proper place, as a tool for your soul. The ego has a history, and baggage, a lot of attachment to the identity that it has created for itself; which is to say that you, identifying yourself as your ego, have created for yourself.

I learnt about 25 years ago that it's important to live as a soul, instead of as an ego. My ego still has a life of its own and will assert itself pretty vociferously. However, I'm much more likely nowadays to recognize that it's simply my ego misbehaving, and I can see what it's doing, and override it when it's telling me something that's inappropriate.

For example when I'm making a video my ego is sitting there wondering whether I'm looking good. My soul will say to it, what the heck, what's important is whether I'm teaching people something useful, and what I'm looking like isn't important. Yet I'll still put some effort into looking okay; is that ego or is it sensible that I look presentable? That's the kind of dynamic between the ego and the soul which still persists and can be useful; and it's not appropriate to put the ego away in a box and lock it up forever. The ego needs to be honored as a useful tool.

So you need to know the difference between what your ego is doing and what your soul is doing, and give preference to the soul, in which you can have a lot more confidence. You will also find it a great relief to let go of the fears of the ego; it can be so debilitating when your ego feels itself under threat. It should have appropriate fears, to keep you safe; but fearing that you will be criticized is not appropriate; if someone's criticism is justified, simply learn from it; if you know that someone's criticism is not justified, take no notice, don't let your ego feel insulted, belittled or hurt; that's simply not appropriate.

So develop a healthy ego, and a healthy relationship between your ego and your soul. Put your soul in the driving seat. And let it drive you with love, which is how it drives.

That part of you that is soul has a life of its own too, very much so, and you need to learn what your life as a soul is all about. You can do this by paying a lot of attention to what your soul is doing in this life, your life. You can do this by looking at your life as a whole, and seeing the direction of your life which your soul may be guiding you along; and listening to the quiet voice within, which speaks to you as your thoughts, whether in your everyday life, or deep meditation or in dreams; your intuitions, your feelings, and by calling for your attention in all sorts of ways; for example if you find your attention suddenly drawn to something, for example something that's happening in your body, or in your surroundings, on TV or in the newspaper, then you might wonder if your soul is drawing your attention for some reason. And a thought might pop into your mind that tells you something useful.

So start learning how to listen to your soul, and start developing a relationship with the universe, or the creator, or Cosmic Creative Intelligence, whatever you choose to call it.

And as for the universe, or whoever or whatever you think of as its creator, this is who or what we pray to, isn't it, or to someone whom we believe can answer our prayers, such as Jesus in the case of Christians; we can hear or see the answers to our prayers, or questions, if we will seek and we will find.

We need to develop a close and healthy relationship with the universe if we are to fulfill our potential as a loving soul, which means discovering fully who we are, recognizing how powerful we are, and becoming the means through which universal, infinite and unconditional love, and some of its works, can be expressed in this physical, material world. Which means you don't have to call on God or Jesus for everything; you can make some things happen yourself. You are the Christ. You can do all the things that Jesus did, and more, as he said you could. You just need to work at it - with love.

Lecture 4: The Road Ahead

Having recognized that we are a great deal more than we might has thought of ourselves before, we need to get it all together and have some thoughts about where we go from here.
We've got our ego in its proper place, its proper role, as a tool for our soul in this life, in which role it's going to be a lot more satisfied than it was when it had no proper sense of direction or purpose other than one which it created for itself from the illusions of this world. Now, as a messenger of love, it can feel totally fulfilled.

You are now more established in yourself as a spiritual soul, which has a purpose and immense power to fulfill that purpose, which you will do primarily through love.

What will this mean for your everyday life, and the direction you will take on the road ahead?

Actually, you don't need to do very much because, as an embodiment of love, you will radiate your love everywhere you are. You don't need to go anywhere. Everyone will feel your love and will feel the better for it. Regardless of what age you are, young, middle-aged or elderly, you will have a very beneficial influence in your environment. You will have a positive impact on the collective consciousness in your surroundings, without doing a single thing. It's not a matter of doing, it's a matter of being. You are love, which the people in your world need. If it is your soul's purpose to be a loving presence in this world, you could hardly have a better purpose. It is what the world needs, always, and especially at this present time.

But if you feel you need to be *doing* something, rather than just *being*, then by all means do something.

You could, for example, contribute a great deal to good in the world, if you were to become active in your community. There will be lots of ways you can do this. Being kind, doing kind things for people; giving a smile and greeting to someone you pass in the street. Being a member of a local organization. A word of caution here, though, you need to establish your own boundaries. You need to decide how much you are going to do and be prepared to say "sorry, no" if you are asked to do something more than you're happy to do. That's a tough one, because there's always more to do. You can't do it all, even if you want to.

One way of doing more, whether it's in your local community or elsewhere in the world is to contribute to other organizations. Without spending any money, you could contribute to good causes simply by lending your support, by signing petitions or offering some other kind of help. In the Resources section of this lecture I'm giving some links to good causes which you can sign up to online, so that you'll be alerted to new causes that you might like to support.

Some of these good causes invite you to donate money towards them. If you've got money to spare, there could hardly be a better way to use it. There are some fantastic things going on in the world which are stuck for lack of money; the Internet provides an excellent channel to raise money to make these good things happen.

If you want to become more directly engaged in changing the world, there are many opportunities to do that, locally and further afield. Locally, you could start a tree-planting club, for example, as a way to contribute to reducing Global Climate Change or just to beautify your neighborhood. Or join a Transition Network to help create local self-sufficiency. Or you could go further afield by flying to Costa Rica, for example, and help restore the tropical rainforest there, to help reduce Climate Change even faster then you can at home, as well as helping to protect the biodiversity - the animals and birds etc., which have been badly impacted by the destruction of the rainforests, destroyed so that we can have beef-burgers and palm oil, etc.

There are many pressing political issues, and economic injustices that need to be addressed. If you want to get involved in any of these things, you'd need to do some study first. But if you already have some idea of what goes on in these areas, you'll know that it takes a lot to change things without getting involved in some heavy-duty protesting. Or you could get involved in awareness-raising if you don't want to put yourself at risk.

If you're not quite ready to find yourself on TV and in the newspapers, then I'd say, "Join the club that I'm a member of." Not many of us, including myself, are willing to put ourselves in the public eye, though somebody needs to do it.

Love will find a way, as the cliche goes, and it's very true. You will find yourself wanting to do things that before now hadn't even come on to your radar. You'd need to give some thought as to what you would most like to do, and what resources, in time, money, knowledge, support from others, and so on, you can draw upon to support that kind of aspiration, or intention.

I'd refer you back to the lecture on "The Law of Attraction" to help guide you in what you would like to do.

The road ahead is long but it begins with a single step; and, as the man said, "Well begun is half done". Cliches, so many cliches. But so true.

Guided by love, you will find the going easy.

And if love be with you, who can be against you?

Resources:

Good causes worth considering supporting:

(with info copied from the respective websites)

Avaaz https://avaaz.org

Avaaz is a global web movement to bring people-powered politics to decision-making everywhere.

Over 40 million members worldwide.

Over 200,000 actions taken worldwide since January '07 About 200 countries having Avaaz members.

Avaaz—meaning "voice" in several European, Middle Eastern and Asian languages— launched in 2007 with a simple democratic mission: organize citizens of all nations to close the gap between the world we have and the world most people everywhere want.

Avaaz empowers millions of people from all walks of life to take action on pressing global, regional and national issues, from corruption and poverty to conflict and climate change. Our model of internet organizing allows thousands of individual efforts, however small, to be rapidly combined into a powerful collective force.

The Avaaz community campaigns in 15 languages, served by a core team on 6 continents and thousands of volunteers. We take action -- signing petitions, funding media campaigns and direct actions, emailing, calling and lobbying governments, and organizing "offline" protests and events -- to ensure that the views and values of the world's people inform the decisions that affect us all.

Causes https://www.causes.com/

Causes is the place to discover, support and organize campaigns, fundraisers, and petitions around the issues that impact you and your community

Founded in 2007 and located in San Francisco, CA, Causes is a tech company that provides people with the platform and tools required to make the world a better place.

Discover, support, and organize campaigns around the issues that impact you and your community.

Causes is a social network for people who want to make the world a better place. It is the world's largest online campaigning platform.

Changes https://www.change.org/

Change.org is the world's largest petition platform, empowering people everywhere to create the change they want to see.

There are more than 400 million Change.org users in 196 countries, and every day people use our tools to transform their communities – locally, nationally and globally. Whether it's a mother fighting bullying in her daughter's school, customers pressing banks to drop unfair fees, or citizens holding corrupt officials to account, thousands of campaigns started by people like you have won on Change.org – and more are winning every week.

We live in an amazing time, when the opportunity to make a difference is greater than ever before. Gathering people behind a cause used to be difficult, requiring lots of time, money, and a complex infrastructure. But technology has made us more connected than ever.

Kickstarter https://www.kickstarter.com/about

Kickstarter is a way to fund creative projects.

Kickstarter is a home for everything from films, games, and music to art, design, and technology. Kickstarter is full of projects, big and small, that are brought to life through the direct support of people like you. Since our launch in 2009, **8.4 million people** have pledged more than **$1.7 billion**, funding **83,000** creative projects. Thousands of creative projects are raising funds on Kickstarter right now.

GlobalGiving https://www.globalgiving.org/

The world is full of problems. GlobalGiving is full of solutions.

Solutions run by innovative, grassroots projects and organizations that are working to educate children, feed the hungry, build houses, train women (and men) with job skills, and hundreds of other amazing things.

GlobalGiving is a charity fundraising web site that gives social entrepreneurs and non-profits from anywhere in the world a chance to raise the money that they need to improve their communities. Since 2002, GlobalGiving has raised $170,942,263 from 431,204 donors who have supported 11,994 projects.

Lecture 5: You, As The Embodiment Of Love

You've always been on a journey. As a spiritual soul you have always been on a journey which is towards expanding your horizons, becoming more aware of what life is about, becoming more competent in life, and contributing more to the unfolding of life in all its potentials.

In this lifetime you may not have been very aware of this, though you're aware that you're always learning, even though you may not be at school any more. We never stop learning.

The journey, or process of learning and gaining experience and competence is one which normally proceeds in fits and starts, and usually fairly slowly through one's life. However, one can more consciously and deliberately, make the journey go faster, in leaps and bounds.

When you decided to learn to love more, you accelerated your journey immensely. Mainly, you are increasing your competence in the spiritual dimension of life. Love comes from the spirit and is part of your being, a big part of your spiritual being. So you are journeying now in the spiritual dimension of your life, learning about it and becoming competent with it.

You already had a good sense that you are a member of your family, a member of your community, of your nation, a member of humanity living on a planet in a solar system, which is in a galaxy, which is one of many, many galaxies in a universe. As you discovered the reality of these things your frame of reference for yourself expanded, and your mind expanded, and your competence to live in this greater frame of reference expanded.

You also had some sense, from what you were taught in your religion, or have heard about, or read about, that there is a spiritual dimension beyond this physical world; but you may not have understood where it is, what it is, and whether it is of any real relevance to you, in this lifetime. You might, though, have some sense of it as another dimension of life that is a frame of reference even greater than the physical universe, which you have yet to learn about, have experience of, and gain some competence in.

Equally, if we go in the other direction, we know there are smaller and smaller things in the universe such as molecules and atoms and even smaller things which only scientists know much about. These things do, however, help us to understand how the physical universe works. And now, through the scientific understanding which has been developed only over the last century or so, we can see that there is nothing beyond the smallest particle other than pure energy and, presumably, some intelligence, call it what you will, that gave rise to this whole universe. In other words, perhaps, the field beyond the smallest particle is what we might call spiritual just as the field beyond in the universe is spiritual too.

This journey, or process, of gaining understanding and competence in bigger and bigger frames of reference is often called "consciousness raising". We raise our consciousness when we increase our awareness about things, whether we're talking about the spiritual dimensions or an issue, say, a political issue which we are becoming increasingly conscious of, knowledgeable about, competent to deal with, and so on.

People who are interested in consciousness-raising very often talk about "raising your vibration". What does this mean? Well, everything in the universe vibrates at a frequency. Even a stone, or rock, can be seen to have some life in, some electrical activity, even though at a very low level in the molecules of its substance. By contrast, a tree would seem to be much more alive, because there is more activity of life within it. As we go up the chain of life, especially towards the activity of mind, as seen in the electrical activity in the human brain, the frequency and so-called vibration increases.

The higher the vibration, the more one is at a higher and higher level of life, generally, with more energy. This might be energy in the brain, in the heart or even in some of the higher faculties of the human nervous system which might give rise to unusual abilities such as clairvoyance and other things that I don't know enough to speak about.

Anyway, what I'm coming around to is to say that learning to love will give you a tremendous increase in your level of consciousness, and in your vibration, enough to enable your nervous system to work much more holistically, giving you better health and a better sense of well-being, mood and confidence, and positivity, which can't be a bad thing, can it.

I'd go as far as to say that love is the fastest route to a much higher level of consciousness for just about anyone. Love is one of the highest vibrations there is, one of the most exalted energies, capable of opening the heart which is the door to an altogether higher state of spirituality.

This leads to an ever-present joy and a sublime peace, which lead ever onwards toward the highest state of enlightenment, the highest state of being, Christ Consciousness. You think it must be difficult to achieve Christ Consciousness? It isn't so difficult. You need to accept that Christ Consciousness is the root of your spiritual being, and part of your DNA, so to speak, and then start living as this is so, to reinforce your understanding that this is so; it won't be so long before you are actualizing your Christ Consciousness in higher and higher degrees in your outer life.

In the Resources section of this lecture I'm giving a link to the work of a psychiatrist by the name of David Hawkins who developed a scale of consciousness which describes what I'm saying. He too says that moving into love is a crucial stage of personal development, after which "progression into increasingly higher states is very natural and less challenging." This certainly is my own experience.

You are an embodiment of love, though you may feel you have not realized it, in the sense of actualizing it in your own outward life. By taking this step of learning to love more, doing the exercises I am offering, and opening your mind to the new horizons I am pointing towards, you will realize it very soon.

Hawkins stresses that each person has the capacity to have significant influence on the well-being of society by giving priority to the progression of their individual consciousness.

Resources:

David Hawkins – Scale Of Consciousness

https://veritaspub.com/product/map-of-consciousness-dr-david-hawkins/

David Hawkins (or David R. Hawkins) is a psychiatrist who not only tackled years of clinical experience, but has conducted extensive research. His career spans from 1952 when he earned his MD from The Medical College of Wisconsin (established as Marquette University School of Medicine). In 1995, he also earned his PhD. in Philosophy from Columbia Pacific University. In his lifetime, he has founded and led several research laboratories and clinics.

Hawkins extrapolates a hierarchical model of personality development. Hawkins argues that the personality can be described in a scoring system which ranges from 0 to 1000 (0 being the lowest score, 1000 being absolute enlightenment or pure awareness) (Hawkins 2002, 75-85). It is of interest to note that Hawkins argues that objective truth is not only existent, but may be reached and understood by any individual using a technique called kinesiology. By accessing the "Database of Consciousness," an individual may have questions answered with 100% certainty. His research shows that results are repeatable and accurate (Hawkins 2002, 29-30), regardless of the individual who performs the kinesiologic testing.

"On our scale of consciousness, there are two critical points that allow for major advancement. The first is at 200, the initial level of empowerment: Here, the willingness to stop blaming and accept responsibility for one's own actions, feelings, and beliefs arises - as long as cause and responsibility are projected outside of oneself, one will remain in the powerless mode of victimhood. The second is at the 500 level, which is reached by accepting love and non-judgmental forgiveness as a lifestyle, exercising unconditional kindness to all persons, things, and events *without exception.*" (Hawkins 2002, 238).

Read more at: https://veritaspub.com/product/map-of-consciousness-dr-david-hawkins/

Lecture 6: And So The World Is Changed

What the world needs now is love, sweet love, it's the only thing that there's just too little of.

Love, love changes everything, hands and faces, Earth and sky. Love, love changes everything, how you live and how you die.

How many popular songs have told us that we need to love more, that there needs to be more love in the world? A million love songs later, and here I am trying to tell you.

The world changes when people love more. It changes in all sorts of ways, people smiling at each other more, being more kind to each other, and people tackling some of the biggest issues that bedevil our world.

When people love more there's not just more love, there's more sorrow too, because we wake up to how we feel about the suffering we see in the world. We want to do something about that. If we can, even in small ways, we do it. The more we open our eyes, minds and hearts to the suffering in the world, the more we feel it. And the more we want to do something about it. And as we do so, the suffering begins to be alleviated.

It's what the world needs now.

When our hearts open, we become more of who we really are; not only more human, but more spiritual. We develop a larger frame of reference for ourselves, and a larger sphere of influence. We become more responsible, both for ourselves and for others. We become more mature in our relationships with others. And so the world is changed, by one person at a time - by you.

We live in an amazing time, when we have the Internet and our own devices for connecting with the Internet and communicating through it, with friends and strangers near at hand and all over the world. People in the remotest places in the world are getting online. The whole world is getting online. The opportunities this offers are staggering in their implications for how we can get the world to change. The possibilities that wouldn't even have entered our minds, or if they did would be thought to be beyond us to do anything about, are now brought right in front of our eyes, with that solution a few clicks of the keyboard away.

And what motivates us to help alleviate the problems in the world is our love, without which we wouldn't do anything; the problems would simply float away, as we turn our attention to something else to entertain or interest us. Now, though, with more love in our hearts, and the means put before us, we don't hesitate to do what we can. And so the world is changed, not just by the existence of the Internet, but by our willingness to use it to give the world some of our loving.

The more people there are who are loving more, the faster the world will change. The collective consciousness will become more loving, and everyone within that collective consciousness will find their heart opening more. The expression "we are all one" is true at the spiritual level; we are all part of that single, spiritual consciousness that gave rise to the universe as we know it. We can't escape the fact that we have an impact upon, and are impacted by, the oneness of consciousness. So when we become more loving, so does everyone else, to some degree or another. You're not learning to love more and being the only one to benefit from it, you're giving the benefit of becoming more loving to the whole world, to some degree or another.

And so the world is changed.

Resources:

Quotes about love and other elements of this course, from noteworthy persons

Charles Haanel

https://en.wikipedia.org/wiki/Charles_F._Haanel

Charles Francis Haanel was a noted American New Thought author, philosopher and a businessman. He is best known for his contributions to the New Thought Movement through his book 'The Master Key System'.

Spiritual Power

"The merchant who does not keep his goods going out will soon have none coming in; the corporation which fails to give efficient service will soon lack customers; the attorney who fails to get results will soon lack clients, and so it goes everywhere. Power is contingent upon a proper use of the power already in our possession; what is true in every field of endeavor, every experience in life, is true of the power from which every other power known among men is begotten — spiritual power. Take away the spirit and what is left? Nothing."

Subconscious mind

"There is a world within — a world of thought and feeling and power; of light and life and beauty; and, although invisible, its forces are mighty."

"At least ninety per cent of our mental life is subconscious, so that those who fail to make use of this mental power live within very narrow limits."

"Some one may ask: "How can the subconscious change conditions?" The reply is, because the subconscious is a part of the Universal Mind and a part must be the same in kind and quality as the whole; the only difference is one of degree. The whole, as we know, is creative. In fact, it is the only creator there is. Consequently, we find that mind is creative, and as thought is the only activity which the mind possesses, thought must necessarily be creative also."

"The subconscious mind perceives by intuition. Hence, its processes are rapid. It does not wait for the slow methods of conscious reasoning. In fact, it cannot employ them."

"You must first have the knowledge of your power; second, the courage to dare; third, the faith to do."

Who are you, really?

"The "I" of you is not the physical body. That is simply an instrument which the "I" uses to carry out its purposes."

Saint Augustine of Hippo

https://en.wikipedia.org/wiki/Augustine_of_Hippo

Augustine of Hippo was an early Christian theologian and philosopher whose writings influenced the development of Western Christianity and Western philosophy.

"Since love grows within you, so beauty grows. For love is the beauty of the soul."

George Sand

https://en.wikipedia.org/wiki/George_Sand

George Sand was a French novelist and memoirist. She is equally well known for her much publicized romantic affairs with a number of artists, including the composer Frederic Chopin.

"There is only one happiness in this life, to love and be loved."

Lao-Tzu

https://en.wikipedia.org/wiki/Laozi

Lao-Tzo was a philosopher and poet of ancient China. He is best known as the reputed author of the Tao Te Ching and the founder of philosophical Taoism, but he is also revered as a deity in religious Taoism and traditional Chinese religions.

"Being deeply loved by someone gives you strength, while loving someone deeply gives you courage."

"Kindness in words creates confidence. Kindness in thinking creates profoundness. Kindness in giving creates love."

Leo Buscaglia

https://en.wikipedia.org/wiki/Leo_Buscaglia

Felice Lemoerado Buscaglia, also known as "Dr Love", was an American author and motivational speaker, and a professor in the Department of Special Education at the University of Southern California.

"Love is always bestowed as a gift - freely, willingly and without expectation. We don't love to be loved; we love to love."

Christian D Larson

https://en.wikipedia.org/wiki/Christian_D._Larson

Christian Daa Larson was an American 'New Thought' leader and teacher, as well as a prolific author of metaphysical and New Thought books.

"We all must admit that there is more in man than what is usually expressed in the average person. We may differ as to how much more, but we must agree that the more should be developed, expressed and applied in everybody. It is wrong, both to the individual and to the race, for anyone to remain in the lesser when it is possible to attain the greater. It is right that we all should ascend to the higher, the greater and the better now. And we all can."

"Believe in yourself and all that you are. Know that there is something inside you that is greater than any obstacle."

"What we love in others we not only awaken in others, but we develop those very things more or less in ourselves."

"In everything, depend upon yourself, but work in harmony with all things. Do not depend even upon the Infinite, but learn to work and live in harmony with the Infinite. The highest teachings of the Christ reveal most clearly the principle that no soul was created to be a mere helpless instrument in the hands of Supreme Power, but that every soul should act and live in perfect oneness with that Power. And the promise is that we all are not only to do the things that Christ did, but even greater things."

Pierre Teilhard de Chardin

Pierre Teilhard de Chardin was a Jesuit paleontologist who worked to understand evolution and faith.

"Someday, after mastering the winds, the waves, the tides and gravity, we shall harness for God the energies of love, and then, for a second time in the history of the world, man will have discovered fire."

"Love is the affinity which links and draws together the elements of the world... Love, in fact, is the agent of universal synthesis."

"Love alone is capable of uniting living beings in such a way as to complete and fulfill them, for it alone takes them and joins them by what is deepest in themselves."

"Love is a sacred reserve of energy; it is like the blood of spiritual evolution."

"Driven by the forces of love, the fragments of the world seek each other so that the world may come into being."

Prentice Mulford

https://en.wikipedia.org/wiki/Prentice_Mulford

Prentice Mulford was a noted literary humorist and California author. He helped found the New Thought movement. He also coined the term Law of Attraction.

"There is a sense in the tree which feels your love and responds to it. It does not respond or show its pleasure in our way or in any way we can now understand."

Peace Pilgrim

https://en.wikipedia.org/wiki/Peace_Pilgrim

Peace Pilgrim, born Mildred Lisette Norman, was an American non-denominational spiritual teacher, mystic, pacifist, vegetarian activist and peace activist. In 1952, she became the first woman to walk the entire length of the Appalachian Trail in one season. She also walked across the United States at least eight times, and likely more than 20 times. Starting on January 1, 1953, in Pasadena, California, she adopted the name "Peace Pilgrim" and walked across the United States for 28 years.

"Pure love is a willingness to give without a thought of receiving anything in return."

"The way of peace is the way of love. Love is the greatest power on earth. It conquers all things."

Harold W Becker

https://www.thelovefoundation.com

Author of *Unconditional Love - An Unlimited Way of Being*, and *Internal Power: Seven Doorways to Self Discovery*, along with several other books. He received his MBA from the University of Tampa in 1988. He left the corporate world in 1990 to devote all of his time to understanding the nature of our potential and raising the awareness of humanity. He co-founded The Love Foundation Inc. as a non-profit organization in 2000 with a mission to inspire people to love unconditionally. Harold coined the definition of unconditional love as "an unlimited way of being".

"It may be easy to look around our world today and see the appearance of chaos, difficulty and strife. Yet, when we come from an open heart, we can also see our opportunity to love all things into balance, joy, harmony and peace."

"This planet does not need more visions of desperation, fear, doubt and hate - it requires an abundance of love, especially unconditional love, to heal and restore the beauty contained in every moment. This becomes the easier path once we take the first step and begin to share our love."

"The beauty of love is all around us when we have an open heart."

"We cannot change anyone but we can love everyone unconditionally."

"Forget who you were and instead remember who you are.....a magnificent being of love." "It's easy to go with the flow when you're on a river of love."

Mahatma Gandhi

https://en.wikipedia.org/wiki/Mahatma_Gandhi

Mohandas Karamchand Gandhi, who was born and died in India, was given the honorific title 'Mahatma' ("high-souled", "venerable") in South Africa in

1914. Employing non-violent civil disobedience, Gandhi led India to independence from Britain and inspired movements for civil rights and freedom across the world.

"Where there is love there is life."
"The best way to find yourself is to lose yourself in the service of others."

"Power is of two kinds. One is obtained by the fear of punishment and the other by acts of love. Power based on love is a thousand times more effective and permanent than the one derived from fear of punishment."

"A coward is incapable of exhibiting love; it is the prerogative of the brave." "Where love is, there God is also."
"Justice that love gives is a surrender, justice that law gives is a punishment."

Elbert Hubbard

https://en.wikipedia.org/wiki/Elbert_Hubbard

Elbert Green Hubbard was an American writer, publisher, artist and philosopher. He described himself as an anarchist and a socialist. He believed in social, economic, domestic, political, mental and spiritual freedom

"Life in abundance comes only through great love."

"Love grows by giving. The love we give away is the only love we keep. The only way to retain love is to give it away."

"Men are only as great as they are kind."

Helen Keller

https://en.wikipedia.org/wiki/Helen_Keller

Helen Adams Keller was an American author, political activist and lecturer. She was the first deaf-blind person to earn a Bachelor of Arts degree. Her birthday on June 27 is commemorated as Helen Keller Day in the U.S. state of Pennsylvania, authorized at the federal level by presidential proclamation by President Jimmy Carter in 1980, the 100th anniversary of her birth. She was inducted into the Alabama Women's Hall of Fame in 1971.

"The best and most beautiful things in the world cannot be seen or even touched - they must be felt with the heart."

"Alone we can do so little; together we can do so much."

"Until the great mass of the people shall be filled with the sense of responsibility for each other's welfare, social justice can never be attained."

"As selfishness and complaint pervert the mind, so love with its joy clears and sharpens the vision."

Neville Goddard

https://www.awakenthegreatnesswithin.com/40-inspirational-neville-goddard-quotes-on-success/

Neville Goddard studied the Kabala, a Jewish form of mysticism, and he was taught how to use the law of consciousness and how to see the Bible psychologically, thus obtaining illuminating insights into the books of the Bible. He developed a new approach to the problem of man and his relationship with the pulsating world of spirit around him.

"I AM (your true self) is not interested in man's opinion. All its interest lies in your conviction of yourself. What do you say of the I AM within you?

Can you answer and say, "I AM Christ"? Your answer or degree of understanding will determine the place you will occupy in life. Do you say or believe yourself to be a man of a certain family, race, nation, etc.? Do you honestly believe this of yourself? Then life, your true self, will cause these conceptions to appear in your world and you will live with them as though they are real."

The Gnosis And The Law
written by Tellis Papastavro
Published by New Age Study of Humanity's Purpose Inc.
www.eraofpeace.org
Copyright: Patricia Diane Cota-Robles

Quotes from Chapter 31 : Pure Love : The Cohesive Power of The Cosmos

"Love is the cohesive power of the Universe and the most powerful activity in the Cosmos. It is the Power that holds together every electron in every atom that comprises form and it is the one that has furnished for man the Electronic form of his Presence."

"Love created every blessing we enjoy, and we owe to its beneficent power all that we are or ever expect to be."

"Love is a Divine Activity and its Cosmic Fount is the Heart of God. It is released to the Universe in mighty streams of joyful, supernal energy; feeds, in its passing, every created form, and manifests itself as the crowning radiant presence of the Father-Mother God to their creation. As a Divine manifestation, it is the apex towards which all roads lead; the motivating and sustaining power under which God's other Divine Principles, to be externalized by man, must seek strength and competence. With Pure Love as a guiding beacon, man's path to God's estate is cleared and sure of attainment. Love, for man, is the Ultimate!"

"The individual that aspires to become the carrier of Pure Love, must no longer mirror himself as a separate entity, selfishly egocentric, but as a co-operative unit working for the good of the greater whole. Being after his Father's business, he consciously lives as a soul – God-loving and all- inclusive – with his life, having been so directed and oriented as to see all forms as God's creations and the externalization of the One Infinite Power."

"Divine Love is the cohesive Power that moves the Cosmos and our Earth, and it is to that Power that man must turn his eyes, if he is ever to find peace and happiness in life."

Oliver Chase Quick

https://en.wikipedia.org/wiki/Oliver_Chase_Quick

Oliver Chase Quick was an English theologian and Anglican priest. He was one of the leading exponents of orthodox Anglicanism and upheld a position similar to that of the authors of *Essays Catholic and Critical* (1926). He followed systematic and synthetic rather than historical methods and expressed his thought in a modern way.

Referring to *agape*, the form of love with which this course is most concerned, Quick describes this as "in its pure form it is essentially divine." and suggests that, "If we could imagine the love of one who loves men purely for their own sake, and not because of any need or desire of his own, purely desires their good, and yet loves them wholly, not for what at this moment they are, but for what he knows he can make of them because he made them, then we should have in our minds some true image of the love of the Father and Creator of mankind." *(Quick, O.C., Doctrines of the Creed, Scribners, Pub. 1938, Pg 55)*

Dr. Elisabeth Kübler-Ross

https://en.wikipedia.org/wiki/Elisabeth_K%C3%BCbler-Ross

Elisabeth Kübler-Ross was a Swiss-American psychiatrist, a pioneer in near-death studies and the author of the groundbreaking book *On Death and Dying* (1969), where she first discussed her theory of the five stages of grief. She was a 2007 inductee into the American National Women's Hall Of Fame.

"If we make our goal to live a life of compassion and unconditional love, then the world will indeed become a garden where all kinds of flowers can bloom and grow."

"The most beautiful people we have known are those who have known defeat, known suffering, known struggle, known loss, and have found their way out of the depths. These persons have an appreciation, a sensitivity, and an understanding of life that fills them with compassion, gentleness, and a deep loving concern. Beautiful people do not just happen."

"We need to teach the next generation of children from day one that they are responsible for their lives. Mankind's greatest gift, also its greatest curse, is that we have free choice. We can make our choices built from love or from fear."

"The ultimate lesson is learning how to love and be loved unconditionally."

"As far as service goes, it can take the form of a million things. To do service, you don't have to be a doctor working in the slums for free, or become a social worker. Your position in life and what you do doesn't matter as much as how you do what you do."

"How do these geese know when to fly to the sun? Who tells them the seasons? How do we, humans, know when it is time to move on? As with the migrant birds, so surely with us, there is a voice within, if only we would listen to it, that tells us so certainly when to go forth into the unknown."

"There is no joy without hardship. If not for death, would we appreciate life? If not for hate, would we know the ultimate goal is love? At these moments you can either hold on to negativity and look for blame, or you can choose to heal and keep on loving."

"It is very important that you only do what you love to do. you may be poor, you may go hungry, you may lose your car, you may have to move into a shabby place to live, but you will totally live. And at the end of your days you will bless your life because you have done what you came here to do. Otherwise, you will live your life as a prostitute, you will do things only for a reason, to please other people, and you will never have lived."

Brian Cox

https://en.wikipedia.org/wiki/Brian_Cox_%28physicist%29

Brian Cox is an English physicist and professor of particle physics in the School of Physics and Astronomy at the University of Manchester, in England. He is also a significant television personality, considered to be the natural successor to David Attenborough.

"We are the cosmos made conscious and life is the means by which the universe understands itself." "You dig deeper and it gets more and more complicated, and you get confused, and it's tricky and it's hard, but... It is beautiful."

"Our experience teaches us that there are indeed laws of nature, regularities in the way things behave, and that these laws are best expressed using the language of mathematics. This raises the interesting possibility that mathematical consistency might be used to guide us, along with experimental observation, to the laws that describe physical reality, and this has proved to be the case time and again throughout the history of science."

"The scientific creation story has majesty, power and beauty. and is infused with a powerful message capable of lifting our spirits in a way that its multitudinous supernatural counterparts are incapable of matching. It teaches us that we are the products of 13.7 billion years of cosmic evolution and the mechanism by which meaning entered the universe, if only for a fleeting moment in time. "

Claude Cohen-Tannoudji

https://en.wikipedia.org/wiki/Claude_Cohen-Tannoudji

Claude Cohen-Tanoudji is a French physicist and Nobel Laureate. He shared the 1997 Nobel Prize in Physics.

"Quantum Physics is no longer an abstract theory for specialists. We must now absolutely include it in our education and also in our culture."

Michael Jackson

https://en.wikipedia.org/wiki/Michael_Jackson

Michael Jackson was an American singer, songwriter, record producer, dancer, and actor. Called the King of Pop his contributions to music and dance made him a global figure in popular culture for over four decades.

"It is now I see and feel that calling once again, to be part of a music that will not just connect but make all feel one, one in joy, one in pain, one in love, one in service and in consciousness."

---

10. COURSE CONCLUSION

By this stage of the course, you would know that love is a great deal more than most of us generally think it is, even though we already appreciate love greatly wherever we can find it, or in whatever way we feel it.

We will also have discovered that we ourselves are a very great deal more than we generally think we are, and the two, our love and who we are, are deeply connected.

We are essentially spiritual beings, rather than being essentially physical, and love is the way in which our spirit, and the greater Spirit of which we are part, moves. In the same way that we feel love motivating us, the whole of life is motivated by that same love, in accordance with the "As Above, So Below" principle.

It has been important that we identify ourselves primarily as Spirit, as a soul, because in our being a soul, a spiritual soul, we can more readily recognize that we are somehow connected through the greater spirit, which is the one basis for all of life, connected with the whole of life and with each other, and we are essentially the same, naturally in a state of spiritual unity with each other and everything.

Our sense of separateness from everyone and everything, which comes from being physical as well as spiritual, is an illusion, an illusion which is responsible for our sense of separateness, and the barriers we set up between ourselves, and all the lack of love and lack of unity we can see everywhere around us. It's crucially important that we see beyond the illusion to the reality that we all are part of the one life, all motivated by love, all unified, and all wanting our lives to be an expression of life itself, expressing the universal, infinite and unconditional love which is its nature.

Now that we recognize that we have that greater love with us, we need to open our hearts to everyone and everything. This course has offered you techniques for opening your heart. As you practice these, and you feel your heart opening, you will feel not only your own love, but the love of others with whom you're in conversation, or in whose presence.

Also, you'll experience more positive things happening in your life; more synchronicities, more fortunate coincidences, things happening more easily for you. You are tapping into the organizing power that love has. The universal love that motivates the whole of creation is yours to use, and with which you can create as you intend.

So as a consequence of you learning to love more, and recognizing yourself to be more, much more, than you had realized before, your life is opening up to far more possibilities and opportunities than before.

It's to be expected that you will feel better for loving more, that you'll feel more confident, more positive, more capable, more relaxed and more self-responsible, and more self-sufficient in your own personal wealth in terms of what you can give to others in various ways.

It's to be expected also that you'll feel better for knowing more about who you really are, that you are a soul, with an existence beyond your physical body, connected to the whole of life and being able to draw on the resources of the whole of life; that as a soul you have an essential unity with everyone else, and everything, enabling you to get over any of the barriers that we erect between ourselves and others, so you can now better appreciate and enjoy the differences and dissimilarities between yourself and others whilst not losing sight of the essential unity between us all.

I hope and trust that you are enjoying the new perspectives I've invited you to adopt, and you're seeing some results that you feel are directly results of this course; and therefore you will want to continue practicing the various techniques and observations I've offered you.

Thank you for staying with me to this end.

ABOUT THE AUTHOR

Philip Snow

I've been preoccupied with the topic of love for almost all my life. Back in 1957, at the tender age of 12, I articulated to myself, without any help from others, that people don't seem to love each other enough. I thought to myself at that moment, and I remember the thought clearly, "I'm going to spend the rest of my life sorting that out." Quite an ambition for a 12-year old! And here I am, still at it, now 75 years old, and still in England.

Of course at the age of 12, I soon became a teenager, and we all know what teenage boys can be like. Nevertheless, when I left school at 18, I went for a career in hotel management, where I felt I could enjoy giving people really good service - an expression, of sorts, of love.

Cut a long story short, in 2004 I created a one-man foundation called New Living', with the tagline: "Creating a more loving world to help us through to a Golden Age". New Living is still going, at www.newliving.org .

In 2010, when I decided I needed to find a group of people doing the same sort of thing, I discovered The Love Foundation, a Florida, U.S.-based not-for-profit organization. After doing some good work for them, I was invited to join their board of management, where I still sit today, quite actively in various ways, at www.thelovefoundation.com .

In 2015, I produced a 48-videos course 'Learn To Love More' and published it on the Udemy online learning system, where I've had over 3,500 students enroll. This book is, in fact, a transcript of that course. I've always thought that the course would be more accessible in written form, so here it is as a paperback, and there's an ebook too.

So I really do hope you enjoy reading this and you find it's of great value to you, even in ways that you hadn't anticipated.